The Unseen War of The Issachar Seer's Soul

Ken Cox

REJOICE
Essential Publishing

Copyright © 2021 by Ken Cox

All rights reserved. No part of this publication may be reproduced, distributed or transmitted in any form or by any means, including photocopying, recording, or other electronic or mechanical methods, without the prior written permission of the publisher, except in the case of brief quotations embodied in critical reviews and certain other noncommercial uses permitted by copyright law. For permission requests, write to the publisher, addressed "Attention: Permissions Coordinator," at the address below.

Ken Cox /Rejoice Essential Publishing
PO BOX 512
Effingham, SC 29541
www.republishing.org

Unless otherwise indicated, scriptures are taken from the King James Version.

Scripture taken from the New King James Version®. Copyright © 1982 by Thomas Nelson. Used by permission. All rights reserved.

The Unseen War of The Issachar Seer's Soul/Ken Cox
ISBN-13: 978-1-952312-49-6
Library of Congress Control Number: 2021901215

Table of Contents

INTRODUCTION..1

CHAPTER 1:   The Unseen Battle for The Issachar Seer's Soul..............................4

CHAPTER 2:   The Invisible War within The Issachar Seer's Soul for the Mind.............................14

CHAPTER 3:   When a Prophet's Soul is Troubled or Wounded............................27

CHAPTER 4:   The Soul Processing Subcultures of Prophets.......................35

CHAPTER 5:   The Philippians 4:13 Anointing of a Prophet's Soul..................................44

CHAPTER 6:   The Kid is Killing the Prophet............52

CHAPTER 7:   The Prophet's Trinity vs. The Trinity of God.................................63

CHAPTER 8:   Life Lessons of The Unknown Seer........................71

CHAPTER 9:   The Tested Soul That Broke

	Under Pressure	79
CHAPTER 10:	My Soul, My Emotions	87
ABOUT THE AUTHOR		95

Introduction

I have realized in this walk with God that there is always another level. I want to humbly submit the introduction to the prophetic reader as an opportunity to go to another level. My assignment is to share the soul's details at work in the life of a modern Issachar Seer. That sounds nice, but the reality is that the very phrase, Soul of the Issachar Seer, is enough to ignite 'The Unseen war of The Issachar Seer's Soul'.

Upon study, this book will show you that Issachar seer's current generation will be weak, ineffective, and a burden upon him or herself without work. I am talking about the battle within our lives of unseen epic proportions. At the same time, many may find themselves in this manner and not even realize it. The war I speak to you about is not ideal for us to experience for God. I will explain more as you delve into this book.

There is a reason so many prophets never reach their goals or build a level of success. We all must achieve this level. Our inner war for 'The Soul of the Issachar Seer' today needs much self-work. The reality of saying that most modern prophets do not want that work is accurate. We want quick, easy rewards and much fanfare from peers and saints alike. We also want to work only in the circles where no one will ever reject them.

There are pockets of us who are here and there. We are building relationships of empowerment; they require time and trust when neither seems available. We are in such a time now. We would instead rather borrow from each other and never talk or work with each other. Social media has given us a delicate balance of choices, and one of the most prevalent is self-awareness. This mindset is how we identify the soul: through self-awareness.

'The Unseen war of The Soul of The Issachar Seer' alerts the prophetic reader to the status of self-awareness of a prophet's life. That is the soul at work. There is an unseen war going on that we do not seem to realize or even consider. We are losing this war and cannot afford to lose it any longer.

Prophets, it takes real strength to get after it every day in the face of the rejections of both the world and body of Christ rejections. Prophets, I have learned that any worthwhile achievement of life requires strength. We need physical strength to endure the long road to get there, so we must take care of ourselves. We also need mental strength to rise from every rejection along the journey. Our spiritual strength is necessary to understand that your purpose is worth pursuing.

Weak prophets do not hoist your championship trophies in the Body of Christ. Those trophies are bolstered only by prophets who have paid and are willing to pay the price for God's purposes. As you read this book, you will know at least one thing: it was written by a prophet who is ready to win championships for Christ. That, in a nutshell, means souls. Our job is hard, but our God is able.

You may already consider yourself healthy and resilient, as it is time to go to the next level of your gifting. Should this mean that there is no one around you, like you, then so be it. God has you in place for this now generation.

Prophet, your strength is something you build every day. Take charge; your soul's health is at stake. The revelations of this book are my most sincere efforts to build the prophetic mantle sent to the nations. I strongly suggest you read my previous book. The Soul of The Issachar Seer" is the prelude to what I will discuss in "The Unseen War of The Issachar Seers Soul."

We, the today's Issachar Seers must elevate our awareness of our souls. This equates to healthy souls for healthy prophets.

Bless you, all! And thank you for reading this book.
Apostle Ken Cox

CHAPTER 1

The Unseen Battle for the Issachar Seer's Soul

How can a prophet or seer be in an unseen battle? The answer is to look in the nearest mirror, and you will see the reflection of a struggle. Unless you come to understand the dynamics, you will find your life in a constant spiral of dysfunction.

Of all the 5-fold ministry gifts, the prophet and the apostle are the most vilified, yet the war for the prophet or seer's soul is paramount for God.

3 John 1:2 says, "Beloved, I wish above all things that thou mayest prosper and be in -health, even as thy soul prospereth." The Scripture is essential in understanding that our soul comprises our mind, will, and emotions.

There is an unseen battle, and it starts with our will. A prophet's will is powerful, yet it is also precious because a prophet has free will. God does not control our wills unless the prophet is willing to submit his or her will to God. Consider how dangerous yet simultaneously powerful at the same time.

There are two things we need to consider. Our will can disagree with the will of God, which is dangerous. The second fact is that your will is that of a free moral agent, with the God-given ability to manage that will. We should consider why our soul does not prosper so often, and we fail to understand the dynamics of what God is doing.

I want to express some fundamental facts now. The will of a prophet is the foundation of God's Kingdom within you. God's administration within your life is your will.

Understanding the source of the battle for the soul of a prophet is priceless. We can now get started to get some understanding and revelation on why we may not have prospered, been healed, or had our request granted by God. We see God's Kingdom established upon this world centered within your will prophet. The burden of your gift is upon you.

As a prophet of God, your will is given to you to be the exponent of God's will upon the earth. The war and struggle start because a will provides you a choice, and if that choice is not in agreement with God's will, then there is a dilemma. You now have a situation.

As prophets, we make conscious and subconscious decisions that will sometimes not line up with God's Word. Our subconscious will live within and below the conscious will. The subconscious resides within our heart, and our conscious will is in our mind.

The conscious will always feed the subconscious will of a prophet. The process is called repetition. Repetition plays a part by providing our wills information to establish the Kingdom of God. First things first, there must be a submission in our will, surrender to God. Romans 10:17 says, "Faith cometh by hearing and hearing by the Word of God." The more we listen to something, the more sent to our hearts' subconscious will by our conscious will.

Have you ever wondered why some prophets and people move gracefully in the word and others struggle? Why does God's Word work for some and not for others, it may seem? The key is to get God's Word into your subconscious mind. The mind of a prophet holds the key to that prophet's success. Our relationship with God allows this unique process to take place.

Proverbs 23:7 gives us insight on what a man takes in, his wisdom of how he thinketh in his heart. The man has accepted it subconsciously, and it is in his heart. The prophet's subconscious will is the heart that may or may not agree with God because we are free moral agents.

Prophets, please refer to Proverbs 4:23-27. Above all else, guard your heart, for everything you do flows from it. We speak what we take in. Our focus is critical, and we take in the objects of our focus.

Guarding our thoughts and considering our paths for our feet, and being steadfast in all your ways is essential. Thus, it is a fundamental principle of a focused prophet.

We have arrived at the essence of the battle within the prophet. The unseen struggle that the prophet deals with and does not even realize many times is the essence of the battle. The question to ask yourself? Who is controlling my heart? Whoever controls your heart controls you?

The devil's ability to get information into your heart is the key to your effectiveness for God. The key to maintaining or becoming a significant prophet of God is to seek and allow God's message to your conscious will and keep getting that same message repeatedly until it gets to your subconscious will, and now it is in your heart. Be aware that this is not an overnight process; it takes work.

Are you a Prophet with old nonproductive habits? Habits you cannot get rid of because repeatedly those habits have been established in your life. These habits are now in your heart, and continually, you try to move forth in your life, but you cannot. It is a small wonder why so many of us choose to move on with the same old habits that strangle us repeatedly.

Your bad temper, your terrible attitude, your unfocused disposition, these are just a few of the many personal bad habits that seem to follow the prophets all their lives. Prophet, yes, there is an anointing upon your life, but some bad habits hinder you as a pure vessel of God.

Let us allow God to deal with us and let them go; the hard part is we can't because we have not realized where they are within our lives. I am laying the groundwork for the battle, so many of today's prophets are dealing with, and we label them as immature, selfish, or not ready for prophetic prime time.

Prophets, can you imagine? You are not thinking about those habits, and the war is still on within and for your Soul. You do know how someone can set you off on a moment's notice with one bad word or one lousy memory. These are serious issues, deep in our hearts, and need to exit from our lives.

Mark 4:24 tells us to guard our ears the physical gateway to our heart. We hear, and we give out and get back what we give. We need to understand that what we give will be given back to us. We are to engage in the process of reciprocity. How a prophet hears determines what a prophet receives.

The level of understanding and persistence of a prophet will determine God's Word's effectiveness in his or her life. The fact is, what we see will determine what he or she can share with others.

The prophet must get the Word of God inside them despite the challenges in their individual lives. The mere fact that God wants us to know Him is the reality of allowing our will to submit to his will. Proverbs 4:24 tells us that the issues of life are in our hearts. Welcome to the work of the Soul, the conscious, and the unconscious, which is our heart.

Our issues are coming from our hearts and what is in our hearts determines our destinies. The reality of the now generation prophet becoming the total of what we choose to see and hear daily is the unseen wall holding us back. I will discuss this concept more in the next chapter.

Should we ever make up our minds to become this generation's Issachar prophets, we should know we have a daunting task within ourselves to accomplish. We must be examples of what we are ministering to God's people. The work we are to do on ourselves before being released to the people of God is critical.

Let us examine, prophets, what is our course of action? We find ourselves in a war within ourselves, and our souls are at stake? No wonder we have not seen the essence of the battle we are fighting. The reality is we do not realize that the war is real. We want to see it on our terms, and the truth is that this type of war is not convenient and certainly not for us to look at to pick and choose.

Unless you and I, the current generation seers, commit to digest the Word of God continually, we will not do what we consider the mundane things of God. These are the things we must do over and over. Things like study, pray, meditate, and seek understanding.

The fact is if we do not, we will not remove 20-30 years of bad habits, attitudes, and multiple other issues not of God that follow us like bees on honey throughout our lives. The battle for the Soul continues and is real.

The mind, the will, and the emotions must work together to be effective for the prophet. The ability to make decisions and understand feelings are clearly in the Soul of the prophet. Do you know why the devil does not care to attack you by conventional means? He desires to attack you in an unseen medium that will affect you the rest of your life.

The Soul of the prophet is an essential part of the prophet's life. The battle of life for a prophet is for the Soul of the prophet. When we see a prophet's Soul controlled, that Soul's won by the controller. The prophet is under his or her limitations and not necessarily always under God's directives.

The winning of a soul, especially a prophet's, is a feather in the cap of Satan. Until you come into a full understanding of this fact, you will not understand the unseen war, who wages it, and how it operates.

Prophet, the attack is not against your Spirit; the attack is against your soul, which is critical and not for debate. Why is this not for discussion? The reason is simple.

The soul is the connector between the body and the Spirit of a man, or a woman. The soul is the prophetic bridge we use, and it yet again is critical in its function. We have heard it was the spirit, but the Spirit and the body talk through the soul.

Thus, the soul is a key to a prophet's elevation or demotion. The prophet's soul receives from the senses (touching, hearing, tasting, feeling, and seeing) and deposits its information in your spirit. Here is the body talking through the soul to the spirit.

Now you have information that you must process. What will the spirit reveal through the soul to the body? Do you see how vital your soul is? The prophet has a body that has a soul and a spirit. The soul transmits information from the body to the spirit. Once the Spirit gets data, it talks to the soul, and that information goes to the body, from the soul.

Prophets hear this. The battle happens when the soul is in this position between the body and the Spirit. When our body does not want to do what the soul says the Spirit has mandated? Thus, we have a problem. See how the soul is in between, and the war for it is unseen, but it is constant.

Our faith and the building of it is a constant process. Romans 10:17 says, "So then faith comes by hearing and hearing by the

Word of God." The body hears and transmits over and over to the soul of a prophet. Information is now sent to the Spirit.

The spirit, which is supposed to have the Spirit of God, will accept or decline information. When the Spirit rejects the information, it tells the soul to say to the body the source of valid or invalid information. The body now is at war with the Spirit through the soul.

The body is reaching out to the soul and the emotions for validation. Welcome to the mental strain of developing as a prophet. You alone can allow your will to become God's will.

The discipline you need, the ability to fast, speak when it is approximate, and act when God calls you to move forth are all covered in this process. Think about it, the prophet who went before his time, saw something, experienced something, and translated that to the Spirit through the soul (mind, will, emotions).

Thus, in turn, data is sent to the Spirit from your soul. The answer came back from the Spirit, and it was no. Then the soul reported this to the body, but the body rejected the Spirit's message, and we go forth anyway, before his or her time.

I have lost count how much this happens. The occurrence of this seems to happen much more than it should, and we all wonder why?

The soul has a responsibility to manage the body. The prophet gets directives from God, which we see passed on to your body from the soul. Now can you see why your soul must come under the will of God as you submit your will? Galatians 5:16 says, "This I say then, walk in the Spirit, and you shall not fulfill the lust of the flesh."

The soul is the feeder for the prophet; we taste and feel the world with our bodies., We need to taste and feel God as we share what God has for the people we have been divinely assigned to by God. The prophet has a spirit that lives in a body, and its connection to a soul must be developed and understood to function correctly for God's purposes.

Control the soul of a prophet, and you will control everything associated with that prophet. We must acknowledge that the purposes of God are to be accomplished, many times in an unseen manner.

Prophets, it is essential to know that we can win this war. The victory we seek is achievable through the soul of His seers, that is you and I. You and I must understand why the enemy fights you so hard for your soul. To process your soul is to process you!

Let us now look at this from another perspective but just as important. The prophets invisible war for the soul of the seer's mind.

CHAPTER 2

The Invisible War within The Issachar Seer's Soul for the Mind

The battles with darkness are real, and they are actively at work in our world as the proponents of "The Invisible War." I previously taught that darkness was a friend because it shows that something is missing by its presence. That is true, but we now examine why darkness wants to thrive in our lives.

Every prophet needs to know about the invisible war. Twenty-four hours a day, we, the prophets of God, are at war within ourselves. The mind is the central battlefield. The mind is the central part of the soul.

War makes us difficult to deal with, difficult to relate. You may know someone else who is a problematic prophet or has had to deal with a troublesome prophet, or you may be that very prophet.

Prophet, before you got saved, you were in the kingdom of darkness. Prophet our war, our struggle, our battle, our hand-to-hand combat is not with our circumstances. It's not with people. It's not with an organization. It is not with flesh and blood. The struggle, or the conflict, is not a material issue, but it's an invisible war. Your mind is the target, and your mentality is the intimate battlefield of your destiny. The battle to control your soul is extremely real.

As a prophet, you must be familiar with Daniel 10. Read this carefully and get the revelation. Daniel receives a revelation that he doesn't understand, so he fasts and prays. And he gets no answer for the first 21 days. And after 21 days, one of the most significant super angels arrives. The angel shows up, and he says, "Daniel, your prayer was heard and answered from the first day, but with my delay, caused by the fact I've been doing battle with the king of Persia."

An angel was doing battle, somewhere, and God was answering his prayer. And something happened in this invisible reality that had an impact on the visible facts. When a man prays, God is answering; there's not only an invisible world but an invisible war. A classic reality and example for us to ponder and study.

Is the battle of our lives ongoing and fought in our minds? We have the temptation and deception to get us to believing lies. The process of being drawn away from God starts. Our hearts are filled with partial truths and untruths. We are in a position to go after a good thing in the wrong way, wrong time, or with the wrong person.

Satan has many schemes. Satan has a strategy to destroy your life as a prophet. He wants to murder you spiritually, emotionally, relationally, and physically. He wants to take you out. He wants to ruin your life, and your ministry. He wants to destroy your marriage. He wants to ruin your children.

He wants to split your church. He wants to have you to be overwhelmed, deceived, and believing lies. To be rendered completely ineffective, as your mind is destroyed.

Most of the time, we see the difficulty in dealing with prophets is indicative. They are dealing with an invisible war. They are either angry or reluctant to move forth, and they become experts at arming themselves with what they consider adequate excuses, and thus they become challenging to mentor.

A difficult prophet is a prophet under all-out attack by the kingdom of darkness fighting an invisible war. God's Word shows us that learning how to deal with difficult peers is a tool of God that will allow other people and experiences to build character in us.

Often, we want difficult individuals to go away and bother someone else. But what if that someone else is you or someone you know well? What is the silent, invisible war they are fighting and do not realize is real? Can you see the reality of your soul?

As prophets, when we deal with difficult prophets or ourselves, it shows that God allows us to be the example of His character. Why? As prophets, we are to be the reflection of Jesus Christ when He walked the earth, and he had to deal with many difficult people.

The invisible war of a prophet is unrelenting, and peace is nowhere to be found, except in God, and the question is why this happens to prophets.

When we look at our greatest gift, our mind, we need to protect our minds from the unrelenting attack of Satan. As a rule of thumb, know whatever gets your mind gets you. Prophets must learn and teach others is how to guard, strengthen, and renew their minds because the battle of sin always starts in the mind. Beloved prophets, how can this be? Do you understand the powerful position of your soul now?

Ever wonder why our relationships are messy and many times nonproductive within our prophetic circles? We don't even know how to greet and relate to each other. Prophets, if humility is the opposite of conceit and selfishness, then humility is necessary to deal with difficult peer prophets and other people properly.

Many of your peers will want other prophets to be patient with their shortcomings, overlooking them, and never being a friend or covenant partner helping them, in love and humility, to get better. They are fighting a silent war that features you as a witness.

Let's talk about hindrances to soul operations. We can start with 2 Corinthians 10:3-5. Here we have the formula for identifying and understanding strongholds. The ministry of torment is put into play here, and the work of the soul is outlined. The prophet's awareness of the prophet's soul is to process everything in his or her life that comes against God. We need to consider every hindrance.

These hinderers that we call strongholds exist to suffocate and destroy us by holding us in a state of flux. The mind, will, and emotions exist to work as one in the battle against strongholds. The Word, strongholds, is a keyword here. It is hard to relate or dwell in peace with a prophet who is beset by strongholds.

God wants us to strive for peace in our dealings with each other. Hebrews 12:14 (NKJV) says, "Pursue peace with all people, and holiness, without which no one will see the Lord." Prophets, regardless of how your peers may treat you, we should try to have peaceful relationships with them.

The prophet's invisible war is simply the battle for the prophet's mind, as strongholds are born by a lack of understanding of the enemy's devices. A stronghold is a view or personal attitude against the Word of God.

Things that will take the prophet from the presence of God mentally are strongholds. Strongholds must be destroyed. They are the stranglehold of the enemy upon an uneducated prophet's life.

Apostle Paul identified strongholds as mental blocks that seek to destroy the 7-Fold Anointing of Isaiah 11:2 and take all our thoughts captive. Instead of our mind being on God, we are now dealing with the ministry of torment. The ministry of torment from Satan is the invisible war's driving force, so many prophets fight within themselves. Each prophet must learn how to deal with this satanic ministry and take captive every thought and imagination, not from God.

The prophet must understand that this life of being a prophetic leader and servant of God is a life that you're living is in a challenging spiritual environment of unbelief, jealousy, competition and contrasting and hurting peers. You are placed in it to develop, display, and become a symbol of an overcomer. Understand the war is invisible, but as real as anything you will ever participate in in your life.

Are we to be strong in the Lord and His might? Yes, we see Ephesians 6:10-20 tells us to be strong in the Lord and the strength of His might. We, God's prophets, are gifted with the armor, so we must use the full armor of God. The prophets of God, we must do this. We need to be able to stand firm against the schemes of the devil.

There is strength available. There is power available as long as we, the prophets, are vital in the Lord," As a prophet, you must allow yourself to be continually strengthened by the power already available to us. That same power that raised Christ from the dead is dwelling within us, but we are not tapping into it.

Prophet, there are evident truths we must adopt. Every prophet makes choices, and sometimes there are harmful consequences. We need to learn not to blame those consequences because everything is not of demonic forces.

The danger for some prophets is that they blame everything on the devil. They always take this approach. Everything does not have to be Satan and demons all the time. We have to be responsible, especially when we have revelation knowledge.

The truth is, we are fighting against a hierarchy of demonic forces to go with our bad habits. The soul is processing information back and forth from the spirit to the mind as this battle takes place in the spiritual realm. Welcome to the invisible reality of the unseen realm. There is a world that you cannot see. It is hidden; it is as natural as touching your skin.

In centuries passed, people could not see bacteria, but it was real and still is evident today. Carbon monoxide, you can't see it or smell it, but if you stay in a room with enough of it, you will die of carbon monoxide poison. The invisible world is real.

Do you remember 2 Kings 6:15? This is the story of the prophet's aide. The prophetic aide got up early and gone out. He sees an army with horses and chariots circling the city.

His servant said to him, "Alas, my master, what shall we do?'" So, he answered, 'Do not fear, for those who are with us are more than those with them.'" In his mind, the prophet's aide was thinking, what is he seeing that I am not seeing. He had to feel that his prophet could not see or even count.

The world that the prophet sees is a real reality. God speaks through him. The prophet knows God. "Then Elisha prayed and said, 'O, Lord, I pray, open his eyes that he may see.' The servant saw; that the mountain was full of horses and chariots of fire all around Elisha."

Prophets, our job is to deal with destroying speculations in everything raised against the knowledge of God. That is what you call taking every thought captive to the obedience of Christ. The battleground for this invisible war is between your ears.

The attacker is the father of lies. He's a deceiver and deluder. His job is to cast doubt on God in our minds. He casts doubt on His Word. He casts doubt on you. He keeps a fresh set of lies. Prophet, Satan does not want you to succeed.

As prophets, we are God's vessels used in the intersecting of the visible and invisible world. We will get the warfare, and it wants to attack our soul through the mind. Prophetically this would be to your benefit if you accepted this fact.

Our souls are at stake. Souls of various nationalities, colors, of every persuasion, of every background, all over the planet, are also at stake. That is what invisible warfare is all about.

How do we as prophets learn how to be that tool of God? How do you teach other prophets the same thing? This is taught by recognizing when your mind does not always cooperate with your objectives. As prophets, we now move in disobedience and rebellion. In other words, a prophet's mind is going one way, other than what the Spirit of God has told the soul.

Welcome to the world of pondering, with its best friend called wander. Have you ever been there when you begin to pray, and your thoughts float away? Welcome again to the battle for your mind, the place sin will always start.

Romans 7:19 says, "I do not do the good I want, but the evil I do not want is what I keep on doing." The invisible war objective is to render us ineffective as prophets and rob us of our ability to fight the battle of the mind. It is the voice of giving up, or it is the same dysfunction of your life again and again.

To deal with this as prophets, we must understand the mentality of being a prophet. The involvement of us getting very personal with ourselves is a reality. Let us get the work in right now.

Look, there are two key things we need to do.
1. Your mind must be renewed and strengthened. You cannot believe everything that you think. The world will overload us with suggestions in our minds that are not of God and false. Satan makes these suggestions all the time; they are called sin. Think about this: our minds are confused (Deuteronomy 28:20). We are anxious and closed-minded (Job 17:3-4).

We then find ourselves evil and restless (Ecclesiastes 2:21-23), our minds are broken and tortured by sin. Let's also look at the subconscious here as Jeremiah 17:9 tells us that we find our hearts deceitful above all things, and desperately sick; who can understand it?

As prophets, we can lie to ourselves. We make bold statements about ourselves as prophets and our ministries to impress others, but we fall into sin by our disobedience. The reality is that if we did what we needed to do, we would be busy tending to God's work.

Let me expand this, just because you get a thought does not mean it is of God. Satan wants you to believe thoughts that do not line up with the Word, and if you do, you are going to implement them. In other words, you will sin. Deception will deceive us into thinking we have no sin. 1 John 1:8 says, "If that is so then, we have no truth in us." We deceive ourselves all the time, especially in our immaturity.

The second thing is we must guard our minds. We need to read Philippians 4:6–8 over and over to get understanding. Read through and over and focus to consider the following. Consider what God says is honorable, pure, lovely, and commendable. The issue is to guard your mind. What we take in will become the basis of our praise and worship. Let us think about these things.

Prophet, focus your attention on the truth that "surpasses all understanding." The unspoken key to moving in the supernatural and developing that mentality will surpass the secular world's understanding. The prophet does not try to understand everything. The prophet trusts God. We, then, have the peace that will guard your heart and mind. We can protect our minds. A mature faith, which is a state of mind, becomes trust. Trust is a protector.

Your trust now walks hand in hand with your prayer. Your mind is now open to "what is true, honorable, just, pure, and lovely. Imagine whatever is commendable if there is any excellence if there is anything worthy of praise." The development of the seer is to maintain a daily dialog with God. The mind's work is necessary for the soul to function correctly. I am speaking of focusing to mature and trust in God.

Focusing is a continuous function for the prophet to be effective. We get the strength to overcome temptation. Allow God to replace it, and it will not persist.

Proverbs 15:14: "A wise person is hungry for knowledge, while the fool feeds on trash." Prophets, learning never stops for a prophet; it never stops. A wise prophet will become a lifelong learner. Love knowledge. Love wisdom. Learn to love the act of learning.

All leaders and that includes you, prophet, realize you must first be a student. You cannot lead if you can't learn. Prophets that want to grow must connect with prophetic leaders who want to grow. The moment you stop growing, your ministry stops also.

Prophet, I have found out that I can learn from anybody if you learn how to draw out his or her knowledge. Proverbs 10:14 says, "Wise men store up knowledge." Our knowledge will increase our sensitivity toward the world.

We must position ourselves to learn more about His Word. Prophets, we must require a need for knowledge. Only then can we get God's perspective on any given situation.

Until we process through the redemption process, prophets have no protection against the fiery darts that the devil continuously unleashes on our souls through our minds. Whatever we have to do, it starts with repentance. We must change our minds.

Are you now ready to make a prophetic mental shift? Do it now, at this moment, as you read, it is critical. We must make the shift as we have dealt with enough trouble in our lives. Has your soul ever been troubled or wounded?

CHAPTER 3

When a Prophets Soul is Troubled and Wounded

Most now, prophets familiar with our biblical contemporaries know or should be aware that Abraham was the first person ever identified as a prophet. Knowing about the development and processing of prophets for being assigned by God, it is a small wonder of the pressure that had to be on Abraham as the premier prophet of God.

We live in a world today of troubles, everything from politics to biological warfare, institutionalized racism, and the degrading of various people's cultures and races. The struggles are real. You know that but you're anointed and still troubled. You cannot help it; you're a part of the world, although you may not be in the world.

Looking at today's times and comparing them to the biblical days, the faces may have changed, but the drama, stress, and the pressure, the chaos, is still there. We can admit it, or we can continue to ignore it. We are affected, especially within our souls' subconscious part, accumulating, and rendering information to us to process and have feelings about situations, whether active participants. These feelings are sometimes unsure, mixed, or totally against a specific source of that feeling.

We all have storms in our life. Some storms we see on the outside, and whether we know it is or not, storms inside us. You can be a Christian, a prophet, an Apostle, a seer, or a watchman; rest assured you will deal with stress, whether chronic or acute. Stress expresses itself in multiple ways, and it specializes in either trouble to the soul or wounding a soul.

Hebrews 6:19 says expresses a particular hope. Here hope is an anchor of the soul. Paul described it as, both sure and steadfast, and which entereth into that within the veil.

God speaks to Abraham and tells him that He is there for him. We can embrace this same promise, also. We must embrace this as the modern prophet. The Word of God to Abraham is also for us in Hebrews 6:14. God gives a guarantee to bless Abraham, saying, "Surely blessing I will bless thee, and multiplying I will multiply thee." We can claim this blessing, also.

Thus, we see God speak to you and tell you that He is there for you, as His present day prophet. He is the anchor of your soul. Our soul is the part of you that processes information between your spirit and your body. Prophet, God wants you to know that he is the steading factor in your life.

The great assurance of Hebrews 6:14 is evident as God spoke to Abraham, and now you can apply this promise to yourself. Hebrews 6:13-15 says, "Here is the promise of God to Abraham because he could swear by no greater, he swears by himself, God says that indeed blessing I will bless thee, and multiplying I will multiply thee." We see the suffering. Abraham, after he had patiently endured, finally obtained the promise of God.

The fact that God has more blessings for Abraham is a concept that Abraham has learned from his experience. He patiently endured. We need to learn from this, and we need to know. Regardless of what we have been through, God has said he will bless and multiply us.

The fact that Abraham would not live long enough to see and enjoy all the blessings that God has multiplied for him is a powerful concept of the reality to the present generation prophet. The truth of the now day contemporary prophet is a metaphor. Welcome to generational blessings, the eternal blessings of God.

God still is the most awesome God. He will do for us what he had done and promised Abraham. Scripture says in Acts 10:34 You have to love what Peter spoke as he says God is no respecter of persons. We also see this in Romans 2:11. Prophets, realize that God made us all equal in His image.

Only God could operate the way he does. He does not show partiality or favoritism, and neither should we! God does not want you to be worried when he says I will bless you, and I will multiply you. The promise of God is a done deal.

Even today, in the world situation with all the issues, are you aware that God knows what you are going through? The central point here is that our struggle is in our soul. We are troubled, some among us wounded in some cases, and our minds are spinning.

We seem to forget that we are made in the likeness of God. Genesis 1:26 tells us that we were created in the image of God. We have dominion over everything. The entire world, and everything over all the earth, and over every creeping thing that creepeth upon the earth.

Prophets, we have to understand that God made man and gave the man a body, meaning God-breathed in him a spirit and became a living soul. We must realize that we have a feeling of and for the world only in our physical body.

The spirit of a prophet, man or woman, does not have feelings; it does not get hot or cold. The body does. The soul gives us the word conscious; we have a spirit that allows us to have God-consciousness. We worship God in spirit and truth. The Spirit of God is talking to me as my soul speaks.

Look at Psalms 42:6-7. The reflection of David as he recognizes his soul. He says, "O my God, my Soul placed cast down within me." David speaks to God clearly and directly as he says, "I remember thee from the land of Jordan, and the Hermonites, from the hill Mizar." The soul is what makes us self-conscious.

The one thing a prophet must-have is self-conscious of him or herself. Will you be responsible for yourself? Adam became self-aware of himself when God breathed into him. Self-consciousness gives us an awakening feeling and responsibility to take care of or maintain.

The soul is critical to the state of being in a prophet; it details his or her mentality. The soul is the self-expression of the prophet; it has aspirations, feelings, and emotions.

The battle for your soul is your battle, prophet, even in these trying times of life. When you realize what the devil wants, you will understand the warfare. Again, the battle is for your soul.

Your marriage, ministry, relationships, world situations, spiritual warfare, and all these things we love to credit the devil for as doing or making are merely tools used against you, the prophet. Consider your soul; think how you look at each of these and more issues.

The wars in your mind are the central part of your soul. The center of your mind is the war for your soul. We serve God with our mind, and the mind is within the soul.

When the mind is troubled, the soul is troubled. When the prophet does not function properly in his or her mind, their soul is moved or unstable. None of the contemporary prophets can afford this.

Psalms 1:2-3 is the reflection of our healthy minds. We delight in the law of the LORD, and his law doth he meditates day and night. Our stability is rooted in our perception of our placement. We are like trees planted in a particular place. We are by the rivers of water, and we prosper in due season.

The mind must be healthy, and the only way to do that is to have an anchor in Christ. When our soul is affected by bad news, a phone call, or a message, we tend to be unstable. Unstable in the sense that we are rocking back and forth through feelings and emotions, and we find ourselves wounded by events of the present and events of our past.

We, the prophets of God, imagine that we are still wounded. Most who will read this are prophets or prophetic people who are adults. Look at us, prophets on the battlefield for God. Do you think any of us are wounded souls that have never healed? The answer is yes.

Are you the prophet or seer who has not healed? We all are in some aspects. The sadder fact is that many prophets never knew that there was a need to heal.

Here we are as prophets, and we never realized that our soul was wounded and never allowed to heal because there was never a reality of soul warfare going on within the prophet.

The assault of the past on the soul, the complexities of the present, and the future's uncertainty make a prophet realize that he or she needs an anchor. We are still human with a complicated job to do.

Has your mind ever wandered back and forth, prophet? And you realize that your soul has been assaulted in your past, now, and that is why you continuously worry about the future?

Many prophets get worn out because the soul gets tossed back and forth and never brings peace or rest. When the mind receives deranged thoughts, it merely does not care, and there is no response to better oneself.

We all have seen prophets, gifted of God, and they are deranged; their minds are so gone until they care about nothing. You are witnessing the battle of the soul. Our war cry for God needs to be heard, and we must and will win.

We must clean up the mind to clean up the soul. There is a reality that if prophets become comfortable with the mess of this world, they accept it. This is a sure sign our souls are connected to something within the world.

We must remember that our souls are the communicators. Prophets, when you can believe that God has given you a promise that cannot and will not be revoked, then your mindset will change. God says I will bless thee, and multiplying I will multiply thee. His Word is so real and undeniable.

This is the promise that I can believe in, and this is the promise I can digest no matter what happens to or even around me. One thing I know is that God is going to bless and multiply me.

Who wants generational blessings for your loved ones? We all do, I pray. Generational blessings will include cultures and subcultures. We will have them.

CHAPTER 4

The Soul Processing Subcultures of Prophets

Culture is an established norm of a group of people. A culture can also be customs or traditions that define a way of life. There are cultures of the prophetic, and then there are cultures birthed within a culture. These are called subcultures. They can also be an instance of thinking or belief away from an established culture. The work of your soul is busy as it maintains your culture and your subculture? Remember that your soul processes information from the spirit to the mind repetitively.

The evolution of the subculture is an ethnic, regional, and economic process. Even this can be a social group. A social group can exhibit characteristic patterns that are sufficient to distinguish it from others within a culture. When you think of this, consider the prophet's role in the Kingdom of God's culture.

Consider the fact that the prophetic exhibits patterns and characteristics not found in the gifting of other gifts in the body of Christ. Think of the soul as the prophet's self-awareness center. The process of how a prophet understands that a subculture is not 'class-conscious' but forms classes because of the prophet's thinking and mental processing.

Let us now define a prophetic subculture as a group of prophets with a culture. These prophets can be different from the culture but still belong to the culture. We should also note that within the subculture, there can be a counterculture. Prophets process information similarly, but each prophet is different. We have our counterculture within the prophetic.

The issue is that there is a difference with training standards existing within the prophetic realm that varies with different groups and prophetic works. Thus, the soul's beauty in the prophetic subculture brings prophets together, similar but still different. We are all affected by these cultural differences as prophets. The soul processes and feeds what we accept and what we ignore.

Our social standards have an extreme effect on this experience; we often feel neglected and do not understand why we are in self-isolation. Every prophet needs to understand this, or you will not grow.

Jeremiah is a perfect example of this. Imagine how he felt neglected and criticized by his family. Jeremiah's time in isolation matured him. He learned how to function within different circles of his society. He knew how to accept God's Word, and his soul learned to process cultural differences as he submitted to God.

The prophet's soul is the central processing tool for understanding one's subculture. You are a prophet, sent to the nations. There are at least four critical issues your soul will process about your prophetic status in the subculture of the group. Remember that the mind, will, and emotions make up your soul. These areas are at work, establishing your culture within the prophet's prophetic subculture sent to the nations.

1. Your soul must deal with different people. Examples are negative or ambivalent relations with other ministers' peers or Christians. They may not understand the prophet or the prophet's mission. They may have been hurt by what they considered real prophetic ministry in their past. Your task is from God. Your mission will involve different people who will feel differently about your separate ways. The prophet sent to the nations must process and discern through the soul now more than ever.

2. The soul is the feeder of your pace on the journey. God will use divine connections and divine associations. They will dictate your journey of being sent to the nations. Many times,

you will be a loaner in your area where you live. Thus your soul can use that time to process information on you personally as you prepare for your next assignment. The processing of this group within your life is a counterculture within the subculture of your prophetic mantle. Here the group is a local subculture that you may relate to your peers dealing with the same process in other areas. This subculture may have you as a loaner within your hometown, yet you must maintain and prepare.

3. Your soul maintains your prophetic integrity. The status you may enjoy with your peers may vary from peer to peer. The nature of this may be exciting in the local area. Your soul manages and navigates through sporadic offerings of friendship and others merely hating on you. You will discern the secret unspoken jealousy. There will always be issues and your past mistakes that your local peers and others in the body of Christ often feel the need to remind you of continually.

They see you and ask God why you and not them? Mark 6:4 says, "The prophet is not without honor, except in his own country. Among his kin and in his own house." Our soul will deal with the exaggeration in hater's minds. Your soul will process how to relate to your haters those who don't understand your assignment. Keep this in mind as you think of the times when you were mistreated and misunderstood. Your soul will awaken you to who you are.

4. The soul of the prophet operates through a refusal to adhere to the day-to-day regularity of ordinary life. Your soul mentality has awakened you to be different, and your self-acceptance

is in process, or it is not. The fact that you want more of God is disturbing to others, not of your subculture.

We demand more of God within ourselves and others who come into our lives for seasons or reasons. Our many prophetic subcultures provide a wide variety that entices and influences the present generation and emerging prophets in many ways. What standard are we setting in a world currently dominated by disrespect, indignity, and even the destruction of the physical body?

The most effective subculture in destroying prophets of this generation is the subculture of nonbelief. We do not believe in responsibility or accountability. Do you think our mentality is ready to accept this fact? We act on what we believe. Our soul fails to process our blemishes and issues. Our ability to have a full life with God is nonexistent.

I have listed four key issues your soul will deal with as a member of a subculture of Prophets sent to the nations. How does a prophet handle various subcultures? The answer is simple. The principles of God's word rise higher than any other culture or subculture.

We are new creatures in Christ. When we grow and mature, you will see the prophetic changes in your manner of living. The newfound maturity transports you into a new and different culture, most notability subculture.

Prophets, we know we are not to be conformed to this world, its culture, and sounds. The soul is clearly at work. Has the soul committed and submitted? Check the prophet's subculture, and you will see what the established culture is in that prophet's life.

Our inability to tap into needed cultures must be a reality. Cultures of healing and deliverance, as seen in Scripture, are still available. Ephesians 5:27 declares how we are to present ourselves. We are to have no wrinkle or any such thing; but that it should be holy and without blemish. Prophets must understand that no matter what defects of the flesh and life we have, we must come to Christ with them for healing!

2 Corinthians 5:17 says, "Old things are to pass away, and all things are to become new." Funny how some prophets hate to give up unproductive habits. Grow up! Prophet grow from the immature, childish things and into Christ!

In 1 Corinthians 13:11, Paul declared, "When I was a child, he spoke as a child, he understood as a child, and he thought as a child: but when I became a man, I put away childish things." The putting away of childish things in our manner of living. He is showing that he realizes the development of his soul.

These are the foundations of decisions and choices that determine whether we will trust God. Notice that when Daniel had entered the consecrated life. Daniel committed himself through meditation on the Word of God and communion with the Lord; these already occupied first place in his life. The soul of Daniel elevated him into a subculture few prophets have achieved with God.

A prophet's thought life on God is essentially related to the heart, not to defile oneself. Identify this as the foundation of the decisive stand with the prophet's faith laying hold on God for strength that will follow. The prophet's soul is at work as it dictates what is in the heart of the prophet.

Every prophet who goes through his or her process shall find themselves. Daniel purposed in his heart not to be defiled by what the world feeds. He also refused to be influenced by what others thought and did. His soul was healthy, and this is a fact. He was a loaner in the prophetic subculture of his time.

The subculture of the prophetic is a different kind of faithfulness unto the Lord. The separation of the prophet is unlike any other type of subculture. The soul has been positioned by the separation of an increase in true wisdom, in heart knowledge. Allowing our soul to submit as unto God, acknowledge our weakness and emptiness, and cast ourselves upon Him, He will give us the knowledge we need.

The issue of the health of the soul determining our subculture is an age-old issue for the prophet. People have questioned you, the prophet, and rejected you. They have seen the prophet as wild and rebellious. They have seen us moving in and out of denominations and abandoning our core doctrines altogether. They have seen our souls processing us, and that is what they remember. The battle of your soul now is to allow your work to glorify your Father in heaven. The work of allowing your soul to prosper is essential. The people want to be able to get the truth from you! Do you represent this prophetic subculture?

We, as prophets, will define various subcultures that identify us as being relevant. The process of becoming relevant is a popular subculture term that speaks of the ability to deal with the issues and times of the day but still use God as the barometer.

The subculture of being prophetically relevant is that the soul has adapted the prophet to the situation. The ability to understand not to fear hard questions and uncomfortable issues is a prophetic standard.

Apostle Paul was eloquent, "I have become all things to all people, that I might save some. He knew that this was bigger than him. Paul says, "I do it all for the sake of the gospel" (1 Corinthians 9:18). Paul adapted his ministry to the situations of cultures. The prophet must do the same to be relevant. Can you imagine Paul's thought process?

Because of the differences in cultures, there tends to be some disagreement within the Body of Christ. The effective, relevant prophet will consider and respect all perspectives.

The prophets marked with a processed soul will show. God places prophets in a unique subculture for the assignment.

The prophet of today may get criticized and judged. Like the biblical prophets, we are not to judge others who live in a different internal subculture.

It's always easy to cast aspersions on those who live, or minister within a subculture typically looked upon differently. They come with suspicion, and this is what many do to the prophetic ministry. A traditional church or a traditional ministry will be different from an inner-city church or ministry, just like we see in the gift and diversification of gifts.

Paul taught us about making personal changes, even uncomfortable ones, "that by all means, I might save some" (1 Corinthians 9:22). Paul was first of all "a servant to all that I might win more" (1 Corinthians 9:19).

There is a reality of culture and subculture that must be realized in the person first. Apostle Paul showed us this. His soul, as he submitted, put him in a subculture of servanthood. Like Paul, prophetic leaders must reach different prophetic subcultures.

Reaching various subcultures is what we do. Paul demonstrated this as he walked in the truth of the Philippians 4:13: Anointing of a Prophet's soul. Let us talk about that now.

CHAPTER 5

The Philippians 4:13 Anointing of A Prophet's Soul

The Philippians 4:13: Anointing of A Prophet's soul is an essential part of prophetic development. Realize the fact that you will suffer to birth, achieve, and function in a prophetic anointing. There is a role your soul plays in this process.

Philippians 4:13 is a much-utilized statement of affirming and decreeing our faith. Prophets today boldly will proclaim that I can do all things through Christ who strengthens me. What's the cost? This is our concern. Let's not fool ourselves.

The prophet's soul stands as the examiner for the Scripture's merit and ethics to do it justice in that prophet's life. The prophet on assignment is the exponent of accomplishment. God's word, Philippians 4:13 says, "I can do all things through Christ who strengthens me," is a rallying cry of a prophet ready and positioned for servitude.

The term "all things" is a powerful statement of authority. "All things" often sends a prophetic message. That message speaks of being empowered in the knowledge the devil can shoot his best shot. The knowledge that you have something that he cannot stop is priceless.

The prophet's restored soul is the key. Psalm 23:2-3 speaks loud. God makes me, His servant, to lie down in green pastures: he leadeth me beside the still waters. Only God can restoreth my soul; this is a relationship. When this happens, he leadeth me in the paths of righteousness for His name's sake.

Can you imagine a vision where you can see all things work together for the good of those who love God? (Romans 8:28) God is there for us to alert us to the fact that He is ever-present. We have to include what we may consider the good, bad, and ugly.

There has been little in life that has or should persuade you that being a prophet is not a difficult job. A prophet should understand that his or her most challenging personal task is development.

We find our development so difficult because, as prophets, we are on no set schedule. Storms show up, and we struggle because we are nowhere close to being prepared for them. We do not have a calendar to schedule storms at our convenience.

There is no defined schedule or time of how we will develop. We all belong to the prophetic family, but we are different. Life will come at us in showers and buckets of what we identify as life's crap.

We proclaim how unfair life to us is. We gripe, moan, and complain. Our soul is now processing information, but there is something we are missing. Let us ask the question: Is the soul processing all known and needed information? The answer is no.

There is no reality to avoid life's pitfalls. No matter how hard we try, they are there. Unwelcome surprises make us feel a specific type of way about ourselves. We find ourselves treated and tossed in ways that we have never known. We struggle with our calling and the rejection of it. God allows it, and we must learn how to deal with it for God. This is the price of preparing for servitude in our development process.

We can, and we do sit back and decree and declare how unfair it is. We are the present day Issachar prophets, who boldly proclaim how and what God is doing. The very reason there is no soul prosperity is equal to the basis there is a lack of the supernatural.

The reality of our development is that many of us will find ourselves used and abused. We are in numerous difficult situations that we do not understand. We may even ask ourselves how we got here. Why do we ask, is this a part of my life? Your soul now seems to question the motives of God. The soul asks the questions that the body does not understand why it is so.

Our thoughts of self-expression about ourselves create another battle within ourselves. The soul of the prophet constantly questions God: are you there for me? You have called me God, and yet I am broken inside. I have problems and situations that you know about God. Why, God, do you not want to seem to heal me of my issues?

We can ask God how you can love me, send me to your people, and allow me to struggle. Those prophets who understand this will appreciate what I will now share. The reality is that God values His prophets so highly that he allows us to be unfinished but on a strict diet of seeking and understanding Him.

There is no secret that God knows who we are, and as we proclaim Philippians 4:13, I can do all things through Christ who strengthens me. We now become processed for the Philippians 4:13 anointing of a prophet's soul. We now begin to see the ingredients of the strict diet of seeking God and allowing God to reveal new meaning in this Scripture.

God shows us that he can take us, use us, and train us even as the world may see us in many different ways. They can say the prophet is useless. They may even say that the prophet does not exist anymore. They can say what they say. The proclaiming of all things is what the soul must process internally from the spirit and control the body with it. Our knowing, "all things" is included gives us an understanding of the battle for the privilege of operating in the Philippians 4:13 Anointing.

Prophet, how many times have you been without God? Understand, prophet, whenever the enemy catches you without God, you can expect a severe unscheduled storm in life. You have demonstrated that you do not know what the Word of God has for you. Prophets, God is allowing you to struggle; this means you need this process. You may have the weapons to win but do not know how to use them. The weapon God provided at your disposal is useless. Your focus on the struggle has blinded you from God.

Philippians 4:13, does it mean anything to you that God's Word says, I can do all things through Christ who strengthens me? Because he will empower me, I have the assurance; I will be just fine. The reality of knowing that all things are all things is a reality that we spend years learning. When you realize that your life's ups and downs are part of all things, you have a solution to your problem.

Romans 8:28 gives us insight; it says that all things work together for good. Storms, confusion, and drama all work together for those who love God. We all have had thoughts. Why, God, do you not always rescue me from my issues? You see me, and you allow me to go through this?

You can not change people's lives all over the world and have no deposited experience yourself. You understand that yes, all things do work together. The reality of that is You and I can have the ability and the opportunity to do all things through Christ who strengthens us.

We can go through all things that God sees fit to send our way. Allow your process to occur. For so long, we wanted to pick and choose what we wanted to include in the all thing's category. Have you found out that it does not work that way?

We have not wanted to include our struggles, unfair situations, losses, embarrassments, and hidden issues we work so hard to hide. Yes, we have been allowed to deal with "all things" in our life. All things that we can do through Christ even include the events of today.

Prophets, the messengers of God, carry a great responsibility. We must know why and when. We must have answers to tough questions about God. Think about the fact that God has the ability to rebuke issues off our life instantly, and if He did that, we would have no deposited experience. We must be able to explain that.

We want our "all things" category to include all the good things we consider to be a part of life. We seek to develop our souls and walk in the Issachar gifting heights, yet the cost is "all things" connected to our life. The good and the bad, we must consider.

How can we do that when the sheer fact that all things must include our failures. All things have our brokenness. All things include the inner struggles that we allow God to strengthen us.

All things include our broken relationships. All things include our bank account; all things include all things connected to us regardless of how we view them. Our sickness, disease, health, and wealth are among all things.

The Apostle Paul spoke from his soul as he proclaimed that he could do all things through Christ who strengthens him. By now, we should know that he was speaking from his heart or subconscious. His heart had already been fed by his soul. Here, we are saying that there is an inner struggle going on, and the prize is the soul.

The prophet will come to realize that this is a part of our normal development. We are overriding our personalized struggles. The reality is that every prophet has some battle.

There is no way to get to your divine destiny without a struggle. You have to realize that if you're going to be the prophet, you will deal with the prophets' struggle. God requires a deposited experience and a full foundation of what he has put into us. Our problem is that we want to get out of the struggle that God has mandated for us.

The type processing of our soul is the needed work for our next level elevation. Do you want to do more for God? You will need to understand and process your struggle.

The Philippians 4:13 anointing of the prophet's soul is an essential part of prophetic development for an Issachar gifted prophet. The prophet does not have to depend on him or herself. They can rely solely on God. To rely on God means we learn how to grow up and stop being like kids. Read on as I explain.

CHAPTER 6

The Kid is Killing the Prophet

Let's now explore the war for the prophet's soul in another way. The kid is killing the prophet, and this is a present day reality. What happens when a prophet's soul refuses to develop or never mature, and yet God has him or her in a position of power and authority? The complex nature of being a seer, a prophet, a watchman, an apostle is a daunting task, to put it mildly. We talked about that in chapter 5.

Prophets, please understand people will observe you; they will judge you, whether you consider it to be fair is an understatement. Very often, people will not have all the facts about you. You will see them scrutinize you because you are supposed to be the prophet. Those who know anything of prophets expect a standard of holiness from you.

They are not looking to see how you have developed for the assignment. People have no desire to see your soul is processing information from the spirit and body. That is immaterial because of the world. The fact is they have their issues, prophet. We live in a world of: I want it now. Send me now. Send me to the nations, we cry out. The classic cliche is I refuse to wait because I heard from God also, is always in play.

Consider that the surface vision becomes the standard in the world, regardless of it having any substance or not. No one is concerned about your soul at all. They feel you should already be at the place of your announced gifting status. That is not always the case.

Today the prophet's greatest personal battles of our souls are the development of the prophetic gift.

Today's prophets have been affected by the fact that I see it, and I want it right now. I see it, and I somehow believe that I am supposed to have it because it looks good to me. The now day era of the immature prophet is that of a kid's mentality. This type of soul warfare is real and has a direct bearing on prophetic mentoring and education.

Prophet, have you ever noticed how a child is as they develop? Do you have a niece or a nephew who, upon seeing something, will automatically claim it? It is shiny, bright, and colorful, and it grabs their attention, and they believe it is theirs. The development of the soul is not yet in play for responsibility, and that is obvious. He or she is a kid.

There is no sense of ownership, no knowledge of working for it, much less developing it. They see it, and they want to take it. Kids may never realize that the stages of life they are in allows them the luxury of not being penalized. The work of a restored soul is absent. Let's examine this as we have grown physically, but the soul's war is in a state of infancy.

What happens when the little boy in a man destroys that man? What happens when the little girl in that woman is killing her? They have never grown up on the inside, never developed, only they have been available to be in a position of authority, leadership, or even influence. Yet, there is a kid within them that is killing them and those around them. Let's talk about this.

2 Samuel 12 1-14 is where this call to action originates. We look at David, but I ask you to look at yourselves. Ask yourself the question is the kid in me killing me? God has sent a seer and prophet named Nathan unto David. The wake-up call David needs has started. Nathan came unto him and spoke about a rich man and a poor man. A picture is being painted here for David, and he sees what is obvious.

The rich man takes a lamb from the poor man. He feeds a traveler. The rich man would not take any of his lambs to provide for the traveler. He is taking from the poor man who could not afford it. We have a picture of the status of this man's wealth and his childish behavior. Imagine you listening to this, and you're becoming angry, just like David.

David responds to Nathan. He has listened, and he has shown much anger at the rich man. He has heard of his selfishness and how a grown man has acted like a child. David is now mad like any reasonable person would be. This action on the rich man's part is very childish.

David sees the obvious, and he responds. There is a more profound, more critical revelation here that he misses. David fails to see himself. David fails to see Nathan's message was speaking to him about what he had done with Uriah's wife.

David lusted after another man's wife, and he got her pregnant, and Uriah has been killed because of David. What's happening is known common knowledge, and until now, no one has spoken to David about it.

Nathan is a senior-level prophet and seer, and the word he speaks to David reflects the status of his mentality. Nathan says the word of God. Only a prophet of his stature could have stood before David and talked about the word of God with the eloquence that got David's attention.

This time in the life of David, he finds himself as a man who yields much power. You have to see here that a less mature prophet would not have got this assignment from God. Going to David was a big deal and telling him about himself was a bigger deal. The situation is true, especially as the kid in God's leader has not grown up.

The servitude of Nathan never seems to get enough credit. Nathan has a track record of service unto God, and he is known for his service.

The focus here is on two souls. One soul is there to warn and announce God's will upon another. The other soul needs to be awakened and matured to the fact that God is not pleased.

God is not in agreement with David's actions or reasoning when we consider that David had everything, and if that were not enough, God would have given him more. How about that he is walking in power, and yet he has the soul of a child?

He is leading people, and his soul has seemingly no ability to reason. He saw what he wanted, and he took it. He was just like a child. David did not care, nor seem to consider his actions.

David is like us today. He had to know he was wrong. David's soul was in an unhealthy place. His soul has not alerted his will that his motives or actions are wrong. David's war is that even if he knows he was wrong, he did nothing to correct it. God had to send His prophet to David.

The soul actions or lack of actions on David's part are like our efforts today. Are we like David? Look at what his actions have caused? His childish reasoning has cost not one but two lives. A baby is dead, and a man has lost his life because of a prophet who wanted to do childish things.

The seriousness of looking at this and seeing David cost people their lives should be a wake-up call to us. Our actions can be like a kid who knows no better, a kid who has no sense of responsibility. The issue here is that David is now in a position of authority. God has not removed him. We are all unfinished works in the same manner.

Finally, David, as he reasons, says to Nathan that he had sinned. David has to lose something to understand his childish ways. The result of David's childish actions cost lives.

We can explore the fact that David's maturity was that of a child in the body of a grown man. David is the description here of a man who has issues within his underdeveloped soul. There is a prophetic reflection of a grown man in a position of power. The man is anointed and gifted. He is a reflection of a counterculture of today's prophets. Can you see the war for his soul? The war has developed at others' expense.

There is a favor reflected on David's life. God provided everything he needed for him. Even if that had not been enough, God is saying I would have given you more. David didn't seem to be strong enough to walk in the favor that was on his life. Why, sometimes, do we act like kids?

We are grown physically, and yet we do some of the things we do. Is it because of belief? The prophetic blessing of David's life is beyond human comprehension. Claim that same blessing for your life.

All David needed to do was ask God, but he did not. Imagine that God had it for David in the same way He has it for His prophets. The grace of God upon our lives makes us like kids before God. After all, God has done for us, we sink to levels of indignity that we have come to accept.

We now go before God and stand as adults, but our actions resemble spoiled kids. David has sinned, he knows it, and he must take action. In 1 Corinthians 13:11, apostle Paul reflects on his maturation as a man. He is eloquent in the process of moving from a child to a man. The childish things of his life are no more.

His use of the word "I" speaks to the fact that he realizes that he has changed. Welcome to healthy soul communication. There is another keyword to focus on, that is "when." The use of the term "when" plays a different role in every prophet's life. Think about it as Paul did, and when will you move on from a child to an adult?

The question is, when does "when" come? Can the soul answer this question? When does "when" come for the prophet, who is unstable, stingy, and irresponsible? When will it show up for the prophetess who always whines about what she does not have but wants everyone to give to her? This type of soul warfare is rampant today.

When does it come for the watchman assigned by God as a long-distance seer into the future? Do you feel the job is too dull and not enough limelight? When does "when" come for the seer, who is gifted but so immature? The same seer that no one wants to work with can be you because of your unstable ways.

When does "when" come? David was a grown man, a king, with the responsibilities of dealing with multiple kingdoms. David comes to realize that this is an ongoing process of development. Are you dealing with the same process? We all are living this in some unique way. Our souls have to be renewed and restored. There is a kid inside of you that is still under development.

Most of us seem to move back and forth in different areas of life. We may be very mature in one area of life and very immature in another area of life, yet we are the same person. There is a kid within us that we don't want to admit, but the hard reality we are all unfinished.

We want to believe we are finished but have we put away all childish things? The question for the prophet is the kid within destroying you?

Notice Acts 13:22 tells us some crucial facts about David. He was raised for servitude, as God describes His servant. David, as a man after my own heart, which shall fulfill all my will. God speaks of David in a prophetic sense as he calls him a King while he was a boy. In this context, he says that I have found a man after my own heart. Despite the failures of David, just like us, God still had work for him. That's good news for all of us.

You are being called Apostles, Prophets, Seers, Watchman, leaders sent to nations, and you don't realize that God is our supreme source. We must depend on God. God's way in the prophetic is sending mentors/spiritual parents who process the transfer that seers need.

They do this by instruction and exposure to revelation and experiences. The soul has to be submitted. If not, this process does not work. Look around in your circles; you can see that.

Thus, the process of unraveling or developing you within your gift commences. The soul now sits in the middle of this process. For some of us, this takes longer than others because of God's given assignment. Many seers never really understand what a gold mine God has birthed them to be to the body of Christ.

Therefore, the enemy will fight you as you come to prophetic training sessions or schools. Even online, where the technology has taken us where we have never been, we still misuse it, and the kid within us never grows up. Satan will do his best to saddle your soul with selfishness. Can you say classic kid behavior?

We are still doing the same things. We have the same habits, same old immature ways, and actions. We, like David, are allowing the kid within us to dictate our actions.

David sees something beautiful. He knows that it is not his. He does not care who it belongs to; he wants it. He has no regard for man or any order; he is a child in the body of a man. His actions to Bathsheba, wife of Uriah, is not the image of a servant of God.

Like the prophet, people were watching David. He had no time to mature; before he took the position. He was on the job, and he did not consult God for what he wanted and get instruction from God. Notice that God says through Nathan that the son he had with Bathsheba would die. The soul of David had been through much, and yet there was still much to learn.

David goes on a fast and prays; he also repents, as he pleads for his son's life. The son represented what had to be removed from David's life for him to move through the process of maturity. How many times do we have to lose something for God to get our attention? David learned a lesson in leadership. The kid within David could have destroyed him.

Notice that kids do best when there is someone to let them know that they believe in them. The critical element of the requirement is a balance in our lives. I'm speaking of the balance between the prophet and the kid in us. We can have fun and enjoy life. There has to be a balance we must achieve. The relationship we must have with Christ as His mouthpieces and servants is critical.

The prophet must have a balance that must be maintained. The soul must be the scale of your life. You must know that your kiddish behavior will destroy all your work; it will kill you because it is the dominant behavior in your life. Those of you who are struggling to grow your spirit-man find yourselves dealing with this now!

Prophets do not let the kid in you destroy the gift in you! Allow yourself to be accountable. David learned the lesson. Stop judging people and pray for them. David could see others' sins, but like most prophets, he could not see his sins. We can be experts on everybody's soul but ours.

That is why God sent a prophet to him. Understand that when you can be accountable to someone, the kid can be managed and groomed, and developed within you. Please do not allow the kid in you to kill the prophet or the gift within you!

This is so critical because as the prophet, you're called to walk in your personal Trinity with the God Trinity. What does your soul do? Let's find out.

CHAPTER 7

The Prophets Trinity vs. The Trinity of God

The Trinity of God is the Father, Son, and Holy Ghost. The Trinity of a prophet is that of a body, spirit, and a soul. The soul is the connector between the trinities. Our soul has to be guided, corrected, and connected for any prosperity to flow in a prophet's life.

The revelation of Matthew 13:19 says we can hear the word of God, and if we do not understand it, there is an open gateway for Satan. The wicked one can take the seed that sowed in our hearts. He now flavors what's sowed with his seeds of demonic oppression.

The seed that lives in your heart is part of the work of your soul. The conscious feeding your unconscious that dwells in your heart. Are you aware of what Satan has stolen from you because you failed to get understanding? The prophet or seer has total responsibility to get a complete understanding. There is to be no debate here; understanding is critical.

We have omitted Matthew 13:19 and have not understood the relevance of this scripture. Could it be that most of our lives, we have tried to correct our spirits when the issue is our soul? Where is our prosperity? Where is the promise of God? How many times have we done all we know to do and still do not have any of the promises of God? We need to know why?

Can we imagine? We have the promises of God and yet do not understand it. We have spent lifetimes dealing with our spirit when the issue was our soul. The soul is being robbed and short-changed, and the prophet is not a reflection of the trinity. We are losing in an unseen war that we often ignore or cannot imagine exists.

The soul is the connector for the God Trinity to be able to communicate with the prophet. When there is no connection, the ability to do anything is useless. What a prophet hears, sees, or thinks is affected by his or her soul's activity. The enemy will affect you, not through your spirit but your soul.

In Luke 15: 11-31, we see the story of the prodigal son. The older son who was there with his father demonstrates an old problem we see in prophets. A closer look at this son, you will see he did not know who he was. He had no idea what he had and was in a place where his mind exposed his soul status. We can see how threatened he was.

Let's look at this. The father had to tell him that all he owned also belonged to the son. The reality of not knowing where you stand is a soul issue. He had everything, yet his soul did not understand how important it was to communicate it to his mind.

The older son had a right to his inheritance. He should have known that what was his father was his also. The older son's inability matches our doubt and disbelief of today.

The problem with the prophets, seers, the watchmen gift, and even apostles is the same issue. We do not know where we stand with God. We are unsure of our status in the anointing despite what the word says.

Imagine having wealth and prosperity all around you, and you are not able to claim it. You cannot process it because your soul is incapable. You find yourself messed up in your mind, so your soul is in a dysfunctional place. You are struggling with your soul with no identity because you heard the word, and you could not receive it. The attack is not in your spirit; it is in your soul.

The prophet must know who has joined with their soul in unity.. Can you discern who your soul favors? Can you say that your soul's submitted to the Spirit of God? We must search ourselves to see if the prophet's trinity is in unison with the Trinity of God.

Mark 3:25 states a House divided will not stand. When there is a division within your life, you will not be able to stand for God. The Trinity operates as one. A prophet's Trinity must also function as one. The mind will and emotions must work as one as we do the work of God. The Trinity of God is as one, so must we be also.

Prophets understand the enemy of God wants to break up your trinity. The enemy attacks your communication center, which is your soul. The attack on the soul will disrupt the entire life of the prophet.

When the prophet's soul walks in favor of God, there is a showering of God's promised blessings. Noah, Job, Joseph, even Moses come to mind as servants of God who walked in favor. They were not perfect, but at various points in their lives walked God's favor and blessing.

Romans 5:5 is the connecting word we need to activate in our lives. The mention of God's love is shed abroad in our hearts by the Holy Ghost, which He gave unto us should alert us to an undeniable fact. Let's look at what God can do.

God can put love in our hearts. God can put whatever we need in our souls to get to our hearts. Do we need prosperity, do we need abundance, do we know what we need? The reality is that the Trinity of God can get anything to us we need. Submission to the process is a requirement for it to be in full effect.

Today in our world, we find ourselves in need of favor released upon and into our life. We need the favor of God that comes when we submit to God; there is a release of favor through our souls to us.

The most crucial point to realize is that Satan sabotages your life through your soul. Imagine everything in your life that has been going south when it needs to go north. Have you ever considered why it seems like an endless pit of drama?

Who wants an increase? Who wants a debt-free life? Who wants God's anointing upon their life? When the prophet's soul becomes empowered, the soul must be protected by that prophet as well.

Think about what you are taking into your life. You must be aware that the soul is the communication tool that will allow your life's intake and understanding of the protection process.

Who lives in your soul? Who are you? Do you know? Are you an eagle or a crow? The enemy of God is and will always be the one who chokes the life out of you. That is his job.

Your worry, your shame, and your poverty are products of being blocked and choked. The soul is blocked. There is no protection. The lack of understanding of the Word of God births unbelief.

Let us think of this in the following matter. Let us identify what is fixed and operating in your soul illegally. Over and over, what has been allowed? Things like worry, shame, poverty allowed while you do not want them?

Romans 7:20 tells us that if we do what we do not desire to do, it is not us, but the sin is fixed and operating in the soul. We must know what's sin and how we are to move it out of our life.

We can be saved and have sin fixed and operating in our souls. Sin can have a legal right to be there. Sin will thrive there if we do nothing about it. Satan wants to demonize your seed and knows that you will not inherit the promise of God because he has fixed certain principles within your soul. Welcome to warfare that is real at an unseen level. Do you still want the Issachar anointing?

The soul of the prophet can grieve the spirit of the prophet. We see this so much as our likes and dislikes come to the surface. Most of us live in some depression, and our souls are the storage houses of lack and limitation. We love God, but we never seem to want to stretch out.

Have you ever considered that your soul may not be able to handle prosperity? In John 14:30-31, Jesus spoke of the Trinity articulating that the devil has no place in the Trinity. Our goal must always be a conqueror for God and a submitted soul.

John 10:10 takes on new meaning. Look at the fact that the only reason the thief comes is to steal, kill, and destroy. The only place the thief can operate and do a full-time job is in your soul. When you can identify the work of the thief, you can stop the thief.

John 10:10 offers us a way out of the snare of the enemy. Jesus said I have come that you have life and have it more abundantly. We have an out with our submission to the Trinity of God through the soul.

We become one, and we cancel the assignment of the devil. Roman 9:1 tells us that we bear witness in the Holy Ghost through our soul.

Our sabotage has been through the soul. The pursuit of healthy mental stability is not always relevant. We have, through our imaginations, been rendered helpless. We are just like the older son of the father of the prodigal son.

Can you imagine being him being there and not understanding his position? He did the right things, but he still did not know who he was. Today many of us as prophets and seers do the right thing, and we still fall short.

We pray, tithe, give, and attend service; we are obedient, yet we still fall short. We are victims of our trinity vs. the Trinity of God. Our inability to get our soul to submit totally and protect us is the essence of the lack of our ability to walk in soul prosperity.

Question? What happens when we labor for years, do everything right, get nowhere, no one knows us, and we labor in unknown vineyards of men? Let us now discuss the status of the soul as an unknown prophet.

CHAPTER 8

Life Lessons of The Unknown Seer

As a seer and a prophet, have you ever been disillusioned with people? You have worked hard, and nobody seems to know you or have heard of you. Have you ever had life not work out the way you expected? The reality, we all have had the experience.

Have you ever wondered why it seems the faithful suffer while the wicked prosper? Have you ever questioned God when it seemed like He was not keeping His promises? The promises of God do not line up with your soul. All is not well.

Let us look now at Asaph. He is a great prophet, an excellent man of God, and yet when was the last time you heard anything of him? He is a prophet of extraordinary faith and gifts.

Scripture introduces us to the life of an extraordinary seer in Asaph.

Asaph's life and his work are the lessons of a working soul. We all should follow his lead. The study of Asaph is critical for us to understand the war to become the prophet or seer, we aspire to become. The fact that most prophets do not even recognize his name is relevant to his importance.

Asaph was a prophet, seer, prophetic singer, and composer. He directly communicated with God often. He served as an apprentice for King David. He wrote 12 Psalms, among them are Psalm 50 and Psalms 73-83. Also, to his credit, he was appointed chief of Prophetic Worship.

Asaph the seer, the prophetic minstrel, was the patriot of a family that ministered as prophetic singers and musicians in the house of the Lord for a minimum of 600 years. History will show that his family mirrored the Issachar family.

Yet, while his exact genealogy is unknown, his personal soul management of his gift is fascinating. His visionary revelation was a special gift of God. He repeatedly spoke with God through his seer gift of visions.

Asaph work was an essential job for God. He reported directly to David. Asaph was an outsider as he was a Levite. The honor upon his life to serve in the House of God was a great privilege. He is breaking ground. He is doing what prophets today do.

He was a seer who knew and saw the power of God manifested in the praise and worship of the people he served. His extreme sensitivity to the Spirit of God in word, song, and music; he expressed through his soul.

His soul was sensitive to the creation of an atmosphere that God found pleasing. He was not well known to men. God knows him, and everybody else knew of his work.

See here the work of a prophet who is not well known but does not struggle with it, in his soul. He knew that God knows who he is, which is the greatest reward he could ever have. Asaph does not struggle with his ego.

His dedication to excellence reflects the high level of his gifting. Learn this must lesson for now generation seers, called of God. Imagine an unknown prophet, with an unnamed ministry doing the work of God mighty. What is your excuse now?

This unknown seer demonstrates dedication, being faithful, skillful, and establishing a generational legacy. We all can duplicate his example. Everything reproduces after its kind. This type of anointing is the product of a sold-out soul to God. Let me stress again, he is virtually unknown, and he has an unnamed ministry.

To understand the prophetic ministry of music, both instrumentally and vocally, is a gift within itself. This level of prophetic ministry is born of years of hard, dedicated work.

The soul, as you can see, is sold out to the purposes of God. Asaph is in the background, only seen at certain times, not well known, not even on the front line as some would consider it.

1 Chronicle 16 highlights the excellence of Asaph, who started as a cymbal player. He combined his gift with the trumpets and singers to express joy and thanks to the Lord.

There is also the fact that one of his sons named, Jahaziel, prophesied to King Jehoshaphat. He told the king not to worry about what he saw before him. He tells the king the battle is not yours, but God's in 2 Chronicles 20. A much-spoken scripture by prophets and fivefold ministry gifts everywhere.

Imagine you're anointed like Asaph. You are basically an unknown prophet during one of the most crucial periods in the world's history. Asaph was a model of so many prophets of his time. He was multi-gifted and not out front but doing work that is needed, critical, and to have Jesus himself quoted him in the New Testament, says it all.

The example of the relationship says it all. His work even today has stood the test of time over the years. Should you ask who wants to be like Asaph the seer, many of our prophets today would say, who?

Let us again echo the fact he is publicly unknown. He displays or seeks no position other than the background-position of support to his leaders. He's excellent at what he does is the result of a sold-out soul. The balance in his life is necessary for servitude.

Every prophet who reads this should discern your status versus your ego status with God. The seer Asaph served under two of God's most significant leaders. He worked with David and Solomon.

The experience was and had to be life changing. Asaph was a Levite appointed as David's Chief of Prophetic Worship. He goes on to hold the position through Solomon's rule. Picture this: he saw the anointing of Solomon, the "wisest man who ever lived" up close and personal. How many prophets can make that claim?

To expound on the importance of this prophet is poetic justice. He is in a position that was important to God, and yet the headlines were not in his name. Today we would look at someone like Asaph, and we would aspire to be out front. We would not want to be Asaph, now would we?

We want to be David or Solomon instead of being us. We would look at Asaph's position as a temporary position. The battle of the soul tells us that we are not in the right position.

Notice I said the battle of the soul. The ego tells us that we must go forth and assume the position as we are serving. The cost does not matter. We saw what happened with David. Go back and reread, "The Kid is Killing the Prophet" chapter again.

The healthy soul tells us that we are to give our best to God. We are to excel in our relationship with him. He blesses us with the excellence of an Asaph and demonstrates some important points.

His example to other prophets is priceless. He demonstrates an Issachar gifted prophet in his work ethic and his dedication. He is a prophet who can face challenges and does not stray from his walk of faith.

Allow me to point out that he is anointed and yet flawed, like so many of us. Psalm 73 illustrates his ability to continue to grow in the faith. To those prophets who feel the need to vacate growth, check this out.

The Psalmist begins with the acknowledgment that God has provided for Israel. Psalm 73:2 says, "The prophet Asaph also says he "almost slipped" in his faith." He saw that it looked like the devil was better to his people than God was to him. What a revelation we have here to study!

A question every prophet should and will ask him or herself at some time or another. We look and see the wicked prosper while the righteous suffer? Psalms 73:2-22 speaks to this question, lamenting his position and the weakness of his faith. In Psalm 73:23, Asaph finds comfort in his life, "Yet I am always with you; you hold me by my right hand."

Psalm 73:24 provides that God is always there for us no matter what position we occupy. We need to follow his leadership.

This unknown prophet has much to teach us about the soul's operation versus the ego.

Think about this for a moment; we see the same things that Asaph saw in his time. We need to ask God for the counsel and follow his directive and not brag about it. The promise of salvation was ever-present in Asaph's mind, and it should also be present in our minds.

The bitterness of Asaph is due to the loss of his murdered brother. The prophet Zachariah is his brother, and no doubt, he is angry and upset as he shares his feelings. How many of us have lost someone who meant the world to us, especially in ministry?

Asaph also reflects Psalm 82 and Psalm 75, a disillusionment with Solomon and his realization that Solomon was not perfect despite his wisdom. He is dealing with a critical point in his life. Asaph's development and serves as a wake-up call today as we are so quick to devalue leaders, especially in the prophetic and apostolic.

The Psalms of Asaph contain great truths for every prophet, seer, watchman, and apostle. Asaph is the poster prophet for the soul continuing education of a prophet.

Asaph's example to his family and us shows us how to remain faithful to the truth. Asaph learned the ultimate truth of what God promised. Asaph learned important lessons about the ignorance and impatience of men.

He was able to handle seeing the ups and downs of leadership. Asaph saw great people rise and saw them fall; he was exposed to priceless lessons. Today our society exposes us to invaluable lessons that many of us fail.

Prophets today, allow me to encourage you to pray that you have the gift of worship and the Spirit of Asaph in your hearts. By now, you should know as you have read through this book, the soul and heart are the same as in connected.

I pray, all those who lead God's people in worship would have the same Spirit of excellence, dedication, faithfulness, and sensitivity to your Spirit. You will allow submission of your soul for the anointing's excellence, even if you are unknown to the general public.

I pray that they would "prophesy" on their instruments and voice by the Spirit of the Lord, for all of us, Lord, we want to give you the honor and praise that you are truly worthy of.

We want to walk with you in the cool of the garden (Genesis 3:8) and we yearn to worship you in Spirit and truth (John 4:23). Our souls are open only to your proven voice in our lives, God. Directly or through one of your anointed servants.

What happens when we have been disobedient to God and now, he sends a test that literally rocks our world. Can you honestly say that your soul just broke under pressure?

CHAPTER 9

A Tested Soul that Broke Under Pressure

The testing of a soul is critical. Prophets know you are going to be scrutinized and tested, and it will be continual. Let us look at the topic of the practice of spiritism and our souls being tested.

Prophets look at Leviticus 19:26, a clear directive from God. We are not to eat anything with its blood. Prophets are not to practice augury or witchcraft. We also are not to consult with mediums or spiritists. Every prophet should know God is clear on His Word.

Our souls are to connect with the God Trinity. The test we see in 1 Samuel 28 gives us the account of King Saul's experience with a medium at the city of Endor.

Samuel is now dead. There are the Philistines who have assembled their army. They are preparing to fight Israel. There is much going on even after Samuel's death.

Saul no longer has Samuel, and he is fearful. God is not speaking to him because of his ungodly ways. He is a man in great power and even greater fear. Saul's challenging part is that he has no one to give him godly feedback. He needs a reference point of reason for the situation he now faces.

Saul inquired again, seeking God, and there is no answer. We call this prophetic block. You are seeking God, and he does not respond. It is like losing all of your anointing and finding that out when you need it the most (1 Samuel 28:6).

What has happened to Saul is a process of an eroding relationship with God. Prophets go through this, and we see in the life of Saul how it affected him. A man of power and authority who knew God. Saul allowed his soul to be compromised when tested by his disobedience.

He did not repent. This has to make one wonder what was on his mind. Saul now decides to go to spiritism. King Saul who had previously put all the witches out of the land. Saul looks like a hypocrite.

Saul's in a hard place. Prophet, have you ever been there? The great prophet to the nations Samuel had died. There is mourning for him, and Saul, who had expelled the mediums and the wizards from Israel (1 Samuel 28:3), now figures he needs one. When there is trouble in our soul or God allows us to be tested, do we act as Saul did? That is a fair question, we maybe should ask ourselves. What is your answer?

The test of Saul is like the test of Elijah or the test of Joseph. We all have our ways of meeting our trouble on the road of experience. Dealing with the trials is a test. Where is our mind when we do? What has our soul processed for trouble and forget when it arrives on its schedule?

Where was the mind of Saul? Had he somehow lost his will to serve God and look at his emotions? He was a nervous wreck.

Now we see the man who stood for the Word of God now do a complete three hundred sixty degrees turn. Look at Saul: he was in a place of horror, and not strong enough to repent and trust God.

As he requests his servants to find a medium, Saul has nerve. Did he think they would not tell it? He wanted a prophetic word. He was unsure of his future.

God will not speak to him, and his prophet is dead. There was a medium or witch in a town called Endor. Saul disguised himself, but he did not do a good job of getting information about the future.

He waits until night. He then asks her to conjure up the prophet Samuel for him. The witch sees Samuel. She hollered and called Saul out for his deception. He told her not to be scared.

Can you imagine her now talking about a spirit coming up out of the ground? Samuel now has a conversation with Saul, and it begins with why would you conjure up the dead?

1 Samuel 28 is an insightful read. Every prophet needs to sharpen his or her spirit with a high level of information and a real-world experience. Like Saul, we are sometimes leaders who have lost the ability to depend on the truth of God in his life.

Could it have been his constant ways that God was disgusted with, or maybe he felt he did not need to repent? What was going on in his soul as he was being tested many times. This is the same process we must master to serve God. Sometimes our issues do dominate our thinking, and we avoid what God says. Look at Saul, now God has his attention and look at how he handles the situation.?

Let us talk about this because there are issues of great concern here. As a prophet, a seer, a watchman, or apostle, you must know and stand in the promise of God. Saul gives us a great example to learn from here, prophets.

Prophets, who appeared that day. Was it Samuel? or was it a demonic manifestation or a hallucination for Saul. In the spirit of prophetic enlightenment, let's answer these issues; so there will be no lingering doubt in your (mind) soul.

We must maintain control of our mind, which is only through our submission to The God Trinity. As the mouthpieces of God, we must stand ready to deal with the issues that can cause doubt and disbelief, especially when dealing with tests. We are who we are.

Ask yourself if your mind is deceiving you. Did God allow him, Samuel, to speak to Saul? Or are we to believe that the witch was given the power or could call up the righteous dead? The action here makes no sense.

God's Word has always spoken against consulting mediums in the strongest terms. This could not have been Samuel's authentic appearance. Was this a miracle? The answer is no.

The other issue is that Saul's enemies did not kill him. The prophecy was not true as Saul, instead, killed himself. God is giving a prophetic word to a prophet who was supposed to have been dead.

We all know that the dead do not return from death. To think that this was the dead prophet Samuel's authentic appearance was futile. The issue goes against God's Word. Samuel's supposed appearance gives credibility to the living talking to the deceased.

There is no wonder we have blood brought believers dabble into areas in which God expressly forbids them. Look at what Saul is doing in this matter. His soul is an emotional wreck. There is what happens when we have prophets who will not anchor our souls in God and repent when we sin.

Saul's actions show us just how weak we can be in the face of adversity. Everything that has been subconsciously placed in our hearts, we go against it.

A demonic spirit spoke to Saul. The message was full of half-truths, as did the possessed woman in Act 16:17. She spoke in half-truths also, just like the demonic spirit. The truth was the apostles were proclaiming the way of salvation. The woman's message was filled with what she knew best, that was deception.

The sad part to consider here is that a leader of Saul's status has been tricked into believing that it was Samuel when it was only some type of deception on the part of the witch. This is what happens with prophets as we deal with the ongoing war.

We miss, we fail when we are not mentally prepared because by the time testing shows up, we are exposed like Saul.

Saul never did see Samuel. Remember, he was prevented from viewing what was supposed to be the spirit of Samuel. Even the witch only pretended to be surprised by the appearance of Samuel.

As we read 1 Samuel 28, we can even assume that maybe Saul had some hallucination when he thought he spoke to the dead prophet Samuel. Since he desperately wanted help and he fooled himself into believing that he was conversing with the dead prophet.

The medium's actions only served to conduct fear and doubt in a man already on edge. Was there a reason that Saul died? Plain and simple, Saul was unfaithful and had forgotten how to keep God's Word, as good as God had been to him.

For Saul to even consult any medium for guidance was an insult to God. Again, he was king and had great power and authority. What was on his mind? The same question we ask so many times today.

Did we forget that the dead "know nothing" and have no part "in anything under the sun"? Saul should know that but look at the state of his soul under extreme pressure? (Ecclesiastes 9:5-6). Do we know of any prophets to include ourselves who may have been released to the enemy by God?

Saul, when he consulted the witch at Endor, he was breaking God's command as well as his own. Saul reminds us of one of our contemporary prophets who know better, but still willing to take a shortcut.

Prophets, it is essential to be honest with yourself as you are doing Kingdom work, and it is concerning the winning of souls. You cannot build others' souls when your soul, all you have learned and know are missing in action. Especially, if it is due to your actions.

We must be better as the tests are coming, whether we are ready or not. The emotional health of a prophet is critical to the health of a prophet's soul. Let's discuss "My Soul, My Emotions."

CHAPTER 10

My Soul, My Emotions

God's purpose for emotions in a prophet's life should always lead to an effective change. Emotions are probably the least spoken of members of the soul. Consider the mind, will, and emotions make up the soul.

We should understand that emotions are an ever-evolving member of the soul. They are essential to the development of the prophet. The day you stop evolving is the day you cease to exist. Learning is everything, especially when dealing with the soul.

What is an emotion? An emotion is a complex state of mentality that can be fear, anger, disgust, grief, joy, surprise, to name a few. Look at emotions as a strong feeling, a disturbance, a total departure from your ordinary sense of peace. Emotions represent actions that have not always been reasoned and approved by the mind.

The word "feeling" is sometimes used to describe emotions as a synonym. Emotions we define as love, and the other end of the spectrum hate are reactions we see in prophets' lives in general.

Prophets are incredibly emotional. This can be a significant stumbling block also. Many prophets deal with emotional immaturity, which is a signal for lack of emotional intelligence." Emotional maturity comes only through and by the spirit of God. Your emotions are spiritually connected.

Emotional maturity develops in prophets as servitude to others. Emotional maturity moves a prophet from "the me factor" to having genuine "outgoing concern" for others.

There is another side to this as we deal with emotions, called the "Me Factor." Many of today's aspiring and uneducated prophets are attracted emotionally to the "me factor." You tend to see it in every area of their life. What does it mean? Whatever I do as a prophet, it is all about Me. Your mind says, "you are showcased because of your gift." You may "say, look how God uses me", as you brag.

The "me factor" we see in many prophets will always connect with Satan's persona. Your emotions are running wild, and your mature peers are aware of this in your life.

The inevitable difference between maturity and immaturity is always revealed in a prophet's life. The prophet who will give of himself or herself with no outgoing concern; demonstrates the way of God, and the principle of His law of love will reverse the "me factor."

As prophets, we are instructed and taught to have emotional maturity. The gift develops through and by the Spirit of God as we serve and allow God to take care and bless us in servitude. Joseph, Moses, Samuel, Deborah, Huldah, Daniel, Isaiah, Elijah, and Elisha are classic prophetic examples.

Emotional maturity in a prophet has learned from a prophet or prophets who are already emotionally mature. The war for the prophet's soul is of utmost importance in the influence of emotional maturity within a prophet's life. Learning the ability to look at things from different perspectives is how we experience and learn.

Control of the emotions of a prophet is a critical element in the development of the prophet. The understatement is that the enemy does not want a prophet to achieve emotional maturity. It is crucial for a prophet, and it's not debatable.

An emotionally immature prophet is usually moody and has never learned to control his moodiness. Whatever the dominant emotion is in that prophet's life, we see it. Most people around him or her will see it also.

God intends for our minds to direct our actions. We are free moral agents, and yet we know we can disagree with God. To disagree with God is not to our advantage. A prophet must learn how to agree with God.

The agreement is the key that will connect us to be emotionally mature as we develop the right character. Our character is the prophet's ability to come to the proper knowledge and wisdom and then direct the mind and body into this exemplary course. As you have read this book, you by now understand this is the work of the soul.

A great example of the soul dealing with character and connecting emotionally is the prophet, Jeremiah. He's a sensitive young man, full of deep emotion. He has a self-confidence issue that makes him feel incompetent to be appointed God's prophet (Jeremiah 1:5-10).

Through five kings, he served as a prophet and was a loyal patriot. Still, despite him being someone who cared deeply for his people, he is branded as a traitor (Jeremiah 37:13-14). Speak about an emotional rollercoaster for a prophet. His assignment was impossible without his isolation. The control he was to learn of his emotions is priceless.

Jeremiah not only heard the word; he felt it on a personal level. He tells God a dozen or more times, "They will not listen!" (Jeremiah 6:19 and 13:11). Like today and even in Jeremiah's time, people's failure to respond to God's message cannot affect our emotional state and allow us not to do our job.

How many of us have been in a Jeremiah type situation where people ignored God's message, then God tells his prophet not to pray for that group of people. Jeremiah dealt with this (Jeremiah 7:16). God says, do not pray for the people. Can you handle the emotions of being forbidden to pray for someone?

Jerusalem falls, and now the people run to Jeremiah. They want him to pray, and Jeremiah waits ten days before receiving an answer from God. Emotional maturity on behalf of Jeremiah is to know frustration firsthand. Like today, many people will seek the prophet to know God's will but refuse to obey when God's message is shared with them.

Jeremiah learned how to stand and not be moved by popular opinions or a perceived lack of popularity. The price of emotional maturity is high. We also see Jeremiah as he develops and the issues he has with God.

God speaks to Jeremiah and tells him things that are not of a person's typical life. He is to have no everyday life, and God chooses to use his life as a lesson to an entire nation. Isolation and loneliness were to run wild in his life, withstanding the presence of God.

Emotions are the last thing on our minds when we accept the prophetic calling; we don't consider that our life may be the example of the message that God wants to be communicated to his people.

When we are not emotionally ready to handle it, we fail in an assignment that is tough enough by itself, without our immaturity.

Jeremiah had a very tough assignment, and it lasted more than forty years, growing progressively worse. Could you handle this type of emotional suspense? To even consider it got worse is mind-blowing.

Jeremiah's emotional state was pretty evident to God as he complained about his lot in life. He speaks to God about his parents, family, and his being the brunt of curses. Look at the immaturity of emotions the prophet demonstrates. He is human and not trying to be a super prophet as we see many strive for today as we attempt to go to another level.

Jeremiah's immaturity is shown as he questions God's actions. Imagine as he tells God that his help is seasonal and not consistent." (Jeremiah 15:18). While this is funny, it is serious in his development. The building of his emotional stability is not something that happened overnight. We see the soul's issues and the soul's ability to awaken to a new level of maturity.

Look, this is a prophet called to the nations, and he claims that God has deceived, overpowered, and prevailed against him. Jeremiah has suffered ridicule, reproach, and insults. Further, his peers await the moment when he slips or does something not of God.

The reality of this is that I could go on and on about Jeremiah. His emotion should show us the present day prophets' importance of allowing our emotion to die to God's directives and will.

Today's prophets can learn from Jeremiah's life. As we see from his youth, his youthful emotions echoing his inadequacies.

Emotional trauma was constant in Jeremiah's life and ministry. So many of us should be able to relate to this. He had a loss of credibility when there was no quick fulfillment of his prophetic word.

Jeremiah complained to God, saying, "They keep saying to me, 'Where is the Word of the Lord? Let it now be fulfilled (Jeremiah 17:15)!" Jeremiah had to continue predicting the fall of Jerusalem for years before it finally fell. This prophetic word cost him greatly. Jeremiah experienced personal inadequacy, loneliness, disappointment, and a loss of credibility, but he learned the blessings of trusting in God alone.

Jeremiah's prophetic ministry was a ministry of trust in God. The right emotion and mental mindset for all who are called to the prophetic ministry.

God does not give us selectively both good and bad emotions. Our destructive emotions are the results of the misuse of the emotional capacity God gave us as prophets.

We can awaken our emotional health as prophets or assign ourselves to the same dysfunctional norms, habits, and thoughts.

The choice is ours. The battle for our soul rages as we seek the depths and heights and width of the anointing assigned to our life. We are in a fight that we cannot ignore. The great news, prophets, is that God is on our side.

In the Anointing,

Apostle Ken Cox

About The Author

Apostle Ken Cox started serving God in 1994 after a series of unforeseen life failures. Out of the military and seemly starting life over again, by 2000, Apostle Cox had found his life calling as a Prophet. The challenge of learning and understanding presented a new frontier. Apostle Cox dove into the process and has now emerged as a well-traveled prophet who serves the Body of Christ as an Apostle.

Apostle Cox, along with his wife, Prophetess Sabina Cox are the leaders of Where Eagles Fly Fellowship Inc., a fellowship of prophets and apostle across the USA and beyond who are dedicated and focused on establishing the prophetic gift back into society as they raise up prophets around the country and abroad.

Apostle Cox and Prophetess Cox are available for Revivals, Conferences and Meetings. They have been featured in meetings and sought-after to teach and instruct the prophetic for ministries seeking to learn more about the gift. Apostle and

Prophetess Cox have 3 children and 4 grandkids as of this writing and currently reside in Durham, NC. Contact them through the Where Eagles Fly office at 919-695-3375 or 919-213-1328 or at www.whereeaglesfly.us.

Index

5

5-fold ministry, 4

A

ability, 5, 7, 10, 12, 22, 39, 42, 49, 56, 64, 69, 76, 82, 89, 90, 92
Abraham, 27, 28, 29
abundance, 66
abundantly, 69
abused, 47
accomplish, 9
accomplished, 13
accountability, 39
accountable, 62
accurate, 2
achievement, 2
acknowledge, 13, 41

actions, 56, 57, 58, 60, 61, 84, 85, 88, 90, 92
activate, 66
activity, 64
Adam, 31
administration, 5
adults, 32, 58
advantage, 90
adversity, 84
affirming, 44
agreement, 6, 56, 90
alert, 45, 66
alerts, 2
anchor, 28, 29, 32, 33, 84
angels, 15
anger, 55, 87
angry, 16, 55, 77
anointed, 28, 57, 74, 76, 78
anointing, 8, 44, 47, 51, 65, 67, 68, 73, 75, 78, 80, 94
answer, 4, 12, 15, 32, 39, 46, 58, 80, 81, 83, 91
anxious, 23
apostle, 4, 52, 58, 77, 82, 95
Apostle Ken Cox, 3, 94, 95
Apostle Paul, 19, 42, 43, 50
appreciate, 47
armor, 20
army, 21, 80
Asaph, 71, 72, 73, 74, 75, 76, 77, 78
aspirations, 31
aspire, 72, 75
assault, 33

assigned, 13, 27, 59, 94
assignment, 1, 38, 42, 45, 53, 55, 60, 69, 90, 92
associations, 37
assume, 75, 84
assurance, 29, 48
atmosphere, 73
attack, 10, 11, 16, 17, 22, 65, 66
attacker, 21
attention, 24, 54, 55, 61, 82
attitude, 8, 19
augury, 79
authority, 45, 52, 54, 57, 80, 85
awakened, 38, 56
awareness, 2, 3, 18

B

bacteria, 20
bad word, 8
balance, 2, 61, 75
bank account, 50
Bathsheba, 61
battle, 1, 4, 5, 7, 8, 9, 10, 11, 15, 16, 17, 18, 19, 20, 22, 31, 33, 41, 47, 48, 50, 74, 75, 94
battlefield, 15, 32
battleground, 21
battles, 14, 53
beautiful, 60
behavior, 55, 60, 61
belief, 35, 57

believe, 23, 33, 34, 39, 53, 54, 59, 61, 83
believers, 84
benefit, 22
best friend, 22
biblical, 27, 28, 43
birthed, 35, 60
blame, 20
blemishes, 39
bless, 28, 29, 30, 34, 89
Bless, 3
blesses, 76
blocked, 67
blood, 15, 79, 84
body, 2, 11, 12, 13, 29, 30, 36, 38, 39, 47, 48, 53, 57, 60, 61, 63, 90
book, 1, 3, 78, 90
born, 19, 73
borrow, 2
brag, 77, 88
broken, 23, 47, 50
brokenness, 50
buckets, 46
build, 2, 3, 17, 85
building, 2, 11, 92
burden, 1, 5

C

calendar, 46
captive, 19, 21

Carbon monoxide, 20
care, 2, 10, 31, 33, 56, 60, 89
centuries, 20
challenges, 9, 76
championship, 3
chaos, 28
character, 17, 90
characteristic, 36
chariots, 21
chief, 72
child, 40, 53, 55, 56, 57, 58, 61
childish, 40, 55, 56, 57, 58, 59
children, 16, 96
choices, 2, 20, 40
chokes, 67
Christ, 2, 3, 17, 20, 21, 32, 36, 38, 39, 40, 42, 44, 45, 47, 48, 49, 50, 60, 61, 95
church, 16, 43
circles, 2, 17, 37, 60
classes, 36
cliche, 53
closed-minded, 23
colors, 22
combat, 15
comfort, 76
comfortable, 33
commendable, 24
committed, 40
communication, 58, 66, 67
communicators, 33

communion, 40
competition, 19
complain, 46
compromised, 80
conceit, 17
concern, 44, 82, 88, 89
Conferences, 95
confused, 23
confusion, 48
connected, 33, 49, 50, 63, 78, 88
connector, 11, 63, 64
conqueror, 68
conscious, 6, 7, 9, 30, 31, 36, 64
consecrated, 40
consequences, 20
consult, 61, 79, 85
contemporaries, 27
contemporary, 29, 32, 85
context, 59
control, 5, 13, 15, 48, 83, 89, 90
convenience, 46
corrected, 63
cost, 44, 49, 56, 57, 75, 93
count, 12, 21
counterculture, 36, 38, 57
covenant, 18
creation, 73
creatures, 39
credibility, 83, 93
criticized, 37, 43

cry, 33, 45, 53
Culture, 35
cultures, 27, 34, 35, 40, 42
cymbal, 74

D

dabble, 84
dangerous, 5
Daniel, 15, 40, 41, 89
darkness, 14, 15, 16
data, 11, 12
David, 31, 54, 55, 56, 57, 58, 59, 60, 61, 62, 72, 75
death, 80, 83
debate, 11, 64
deceased, 83
deceitful, 23
deceived, 16, 92
deceiver, 21
deception, 16, 82, 84
declare, 46
decree, 46
dedicated, 73, 95
dedication, 73, 76, 78
defiled, 41
deluder, 21
demand, 39
demonic, 20, 64, 82, 84
demonstrated, 43, 48
demonstrates, 65, 73, 76, 89, 92

demotion, 11
departure, 88
depend, 51, 60, 82
deposited, 49, 50
deposits, 11
depression, 68
depths, 94
deranged, 33
desire, 53, 68
destinies, 9
destiny, 15, 50
destroy, 16, 18, 19, 61, 62, 69
destruction, 39
develop, 19, 46, 49, 52, 53, 90
developed, 13, 53, 54, 57, 62
development, 24, 27, 40, 44, 45, 46, 47, 50, 51, 53, 54, 59, 77, 87, 89, 92
devil, 7, 10, 20, 25, 31, 45, 68, 69, 76
dialog, 24
digest, 10, 34
dilemma, 6
directive, 77, 79
directives, 10, 13, 93
disagree, 5, 90
disagreement, 42
disappointment, 93
disbelief, 65, 83
discern, 37, 38, 65, 75
discussion, 11
disease, 50

disguised, 81
disillusioned, 71
disillusionment, 77
dislikes, 68
disobedience, 22, 23, 80
displays, 74
disposal, 48
disposition, 8
disrespect, 39
disturbance, 87
divinely, 13
division, 66
dominate, 82
dominion, 30
doubt, 21, 65, 77, 83, 85
dove, 95
dozen, 90
drama, 28, 48, 67
dynamics, 4, 5
dysfunction, 4, 22

E

ears, 8, 21
earth, 6, 17, 30
echo, 74
education, 53, 77
effective, 10, 24, 39, 42, 87
effectiveness, 7, 8
efforts, 3, 56

ego, 73, 75, 77
elevation, 11, 50
Elijah, 81, 89
Elisha, 21, 89
embarrassments, 49
emerged, 95
emotional, 84, 86, 88, 89, 90, 91, 92, 93
emotionally, 16, 88, 89, 90, 92
emotions, 5, 10, 12, 18, 31, 32, 37, 66, 81, 87, 88, 89, 90, 91, 92, 93
Emotions, 86, 87, 88, 91
empowered, 45, 67
empowerment, 2
emptiness, 41
encourage, 78
Endor, 80, 81, 85
endure, 2
enemy, 13, 19, 48, 60, 64, 66, 67, 69, 85, 89
engage, 8
enlightenment, 83
entices, 39
epic, 1
era, 53
established, 5, 7, 35, 40
establishing, 37, 73, 95
ethics, 45
evolution, 36
evolving, 87
exaggeration, 38
examiner, 45

example, 16, 17, 37, 73, 74, 76, 77, 82, 90, 91
excellence, 24, 73, 74, 76, 78
excellent, 71, 74
excuses, 16
experience, 1, 29, 36, 49, 50, 71, 75, 80, 81, 82, 89
exposed, 65, 78, 84
exposure, 60
express, 5, 74
extraordinary, 71, 72

F

fact, 5, 8, 9, 10, 15, 22, 29, 32, 36, 39, 41, 44, 45, 49, 50, 53, 56, 57, 58, 66, 69, 72, 74
factor, 29, 88, 89
fail, 5, 78, 84, 92
failure, 90
failures, 50, 60, 95
faith, 11, 24, 41, 44, 71, 76
Faith, 6
faithful, 71, 73, 77
faithfulness, 41, 78
family, 37, 46, 72, 77, 92
fanfare, 2
favor, 57, 66, 67
fear, 21, 42, 80, 85, 87
fearful, 80
feeling, 11, 28, 30, 31, 87, 88
feelings, 10, 28, 30, 31, 32, 77
feet, 7

fights, 13
fire, 21
flesh, 13, 15, 40
flows, 7
focus, 7, 24, 48, 56, 58
focused, 7, 95
fool, 25, 44
fooled, 85
forgotten, 85
foundation, 5, 41, 50
free will, 5
friendship, 38
frontier, 95
frustration, 91
fulfill, 13, 59
fulfillment, 93
function, 11, 13, 24, 32, 37, 44, 66
funny, 92
future, 33, 59, 81

G

gateway, 8, 63
genealogy, 72
generation, 1, 3, 9, 10, 29, 39, 73
gift, 5, 17, 43, 53, 60, 62, 65, 72, 73, 74, 78, 88, 89, 95
gifting, 3, 36, 49, 53, 73
God, 1, 3, 4, 5, 6, 7, 8, 9, 10, 12, 13, 14, 15, 16, 17, 18, 19, 20, 21, 22, 23, 24, 25, 27, 28, 29, 30, 31, 32, 33, 34, 36, 37, 38, 39, 40, 41, 42, 45, 46, 47, 48, 49, 50, 51, 52, 53, 54, 55, 56, 57, 58,

59, 60, 61, 62, 63, 64, 65, 66, 67, 68, 69, 71, 72, 73, 74, 75, 76, 77, 78, 79, 80, 81, 82, 83, 84, 85, 87, 88, 89, 90, 91, 92, 93, 94, 95

good, 16, 22, 45, 48, 49, 53, 60, 81, 85, 93

gospel, 42

grace, 58

gripe, 46

groundwork, 8

growth, 76

guard, 7, 8, 17, 24

guidance, 85

guided, 63

H

habits, 7, 8, 10, 20, 40, 60, 93

half-truths, 84

hallucination, 82, 84

heal, 32, 33, 47

healed, 5, 32

health, 3, 5, 41, 50, 86, 93

healthy, 3, 32, 41, 58, 69, 76

hearing, 6, 11

heart, 6, 7, 8, 9, 24, 41, 50, 59, 60, 64, 78

heights, 49, 94

hindrance, 18

History, 72

holiness, 18, 53

holy, 40

hometown, 38

honest, 85
honorable, 24
hope, 28
horror, 81
horses, 21
house, 38, 72
humility, 17, 18
hypocrite, 80

I

idea, 65
identify, 2, 42, 46, 68, 69
identity, 65
ignite, 1
ignorance, 77
illegally, 68
image, 30, 61
imagination, 19
imaginations, 69
imagine, 8, 32, 42, 45, 64, 69, 82
immature, 8, 40, 53, 59, 60, 89
immaturity, 23, 88, 89, 92
impatience, 77
implement, 23
importance, 72, 75, 89, 93
impossible, 90
inability, 40, 65, 69
inadequacy, 93
incapable, 65

incompetent, 90
increase, 25, 41, 67
indignity, 39, 58
ineffective, 1, 16, 22
infancy, 54
influence, 54, 89
influences, 39
information, 6, 7, 11, 12, 20, 28, 29, 35, 36, 38, 46, 53, 81, 82
ingredients, 47
inherit, 68
inheritance, 65
insight, 6, 48
instruct, 95
instrumentally, 73
insult, 85
insults, 92
intake, 67
intelligence, 88
internal, 43
invaluable, 78
invisible, 13, 14, 15, 16, 17, 19, 20, 21, 22
irresponsible, 58
isolation, 37, 90
Isolation, 91
Israel, 76, 80, 81
Issachar Seer, 1, 2, 3, 4, 14
issue, 15, 24, 36, 41, 57, 64, 65, 83, 90
issues, 9, 10, 30, 31, 37, 38, 39, 42, 47, 48, 49, 53, 57, 82, 83, 91, 92

J

Jahaziel, 74
jealousy, 19, 38
Jehoshaphat, 74
Jeremiah, 23, 37, 90, 91, 92, 93
Jesus, 17, 68, 69, 74
job, 3, 21, 33, 45, 59, 61, 67, 69, 72, 81, 90
Joseph, 66, 81, 89
journey, 3, 37
judge, 43, 52
judged, 43

K

key, 6, 7, 11, 23, 24, 39, 45, 90
keyword, 18, 58
killing, 52, 54
Kingdom, 5, 6, 36, 85
kingdoms, 59
knowledge, 20, 21, 25, 41, 45, 54, 55, 90

L

labor, 70
lack, 19, 46, 56, 67, 68, 69, 88, 91
lambs, 54
leaders, 25, 43, 60, 74, 75, 77, 82, 95
leadership, 54, 61, 76, 78
legacy, 73

lesson, 61, 62, 73, 91
level, 1, 2, 3, 8, 50, 55, 68, 73, 82, 90, 92
Levite, 72, 75
lies, 16, 21
life, 1, 2, 4, 5, 7, 8, 9, 10, 16, 18, 19, 22, 28, 29, 31, 35, 38, 39, 40, 41, 45, 46, 47, 48, 49, 54, 55, 57, 58, 59, 61, 63, 66, 67, 68, 69, 71, 72, 75, 76, 77, 80, 82, 87, 88, 89, 91, 92, 93, 94, 95
likes, 68
limelight, 59
limitation, 68
limitations, 10
listen, 6, 90
loneliness, 91, 93
Lord, 18, 19, 20, 21, 40, 41, 72, 74, 78, 93
losses, 49
lousy memory, 8
love, 18, 25, 29, 31, 45, 47, 48, 66, 68, 88, 89
lovely, 24

M

mad, 55
manage, 5, 13
manifestation, 82
mantle, 3, 38
marriage, 16, 31
master, 21, 82
maturation, 58
meditate, 10
meditates, 32

mediums, 79, 81, 83
Meetings, 95
members, 87
mental, 2, 12, 19, 25, 36, 69, 93
mentality, 15, 22, 24, 31, 38, 39, 53, 55, 87
mentor, 16
mentoring, 53
mentors, 60
merit, 45
message, 7, 12, 32, 45, 55, 84, 90, 91
military, 95
mind, 5, 6, 10, 12, 13, 15, 16, 17, 18, 19, 20, 21, 22, 23, 24, 31, 32, 33, 35, 37, 38, 65, 66, 77, 80, 81, 83, 85, 87, 88, 90, 92
minds, 9, 16, 17, 21, 23, 24, 25, 30, 32, 33, 38, 77, 90, 91
mindset, 2, 34, 93
ministry, 16, 18, 19, 25, 31, 37, 42, 43, 73, 74, 77, 93
miracle, 83
mirror, 4
mistakes, 38
misunderstood, 38
moan, 46
moment, 8, 25, 77, 92
moodiness, 89
moral, 5, 7, 90
motives, 47, 56
mountain, 21
mourning, 81
mouthpieces, 61, 83
multiply, 28, 29, 30, 34
multiplying, 28, 29, 34

murder, 16
music, 73
musicians, 72

N

Nathan, 54, 55, 56, 57, 61
nationalities, 22
nations, 3, 37, 39, 53, 60, 81, 92
nephew, 53
New Testament, 74
news, 32, 60, 94
niece, 53
nonproductive, 7, 17
norms, 93
north, 67

O

obedient, 69
occupy, 76
occurrence, 12
operates, 10, 38, 66
opportunity, 1, 49
organization, 15
overcomer, 19
overnight, 7, 92
overpowered, 92
overwhelmed, 16
ownership, 54

P

pace, 37
parents, 60, 92
paths, 7, 45
patient, 18
patriot, 72, 90
pay, 3
peace, 17, 18, 24, 33, 88
peaceful, 18
peers, 2, 16, 18, 19, 37, 38, 88, 92
penalized, 54
personal, 8, 19, 23, 43, 45, 53, 62, 72, 75, 90, 93
perspectives, 42, 89
Philistines, 80
physically, 16, 54, 57
picture, 54
pitfalls, 46
planet, 22
pockets, 2
poetic justice, 75
poison, 21
politics, 27
poor, 54
popular, 42, 91
popularity, 91
position, 11, 16, 17, 25, 52, 54, 57, 61, 69, 74, 75, 76
poverty, 67, 68
power, 20, 52, 55, 56, 57, 73, 80, 83, 85
powerful, 5, 17, 29, 45

praise, 24, 73, 78
pray, 10, 21, 22, 34, 62, 69, 78, 91
prayer, 15, 24
predicting, 93
pregnant, 55
prelude, 3
presence, 14, 19, 91
pressure, 27, 28, 78, 85
pretended, 84
prevailed, 92
price, 3, 46, 91
priceless, 5, 45, 76, 78, 90
principle, 7, 89
privilege, 48, 72
prize, 50
problem, 11, 48, 50, 65
process, 6, 7, 8, 11, 12, 13, 16, 18, 25, 28, 36, 37, 38, 39, 41, 42, 44, 46, 48, 49, 50, 58, 59, 60, 61, 65, 67, 80, 82, 95
proclaim, 44, 46, 47
proclaiming, 48, 84
promise, 28, 29, 30, 34, 64, 68, 77, 82
prophet, 2, 3, 4, 5, 6, 7, 8, 9, 10, 11, 12, 13, 14, 15, 16, 17, 18, 19, 20, 21, 22, 24, 25, 27, 28, 29, 30, 31, 32, 33, 36, 37, 38, 39, 40, 41, 42, 43, 45, 47, 48, 50, 51, 52, 53, 54, 55, 56, 57, 58, 59, 61, 62, 63, 64, 65, 66, 67, 68, 70, 71, 72, 73, 74, 75, 76, 77, 79, 81, 82, 83, 85, 86, 87, 88, 89, 90, 91, 92, 95
Prophetess Sabina Cox, 95
prophetic, 1, 2, 3, 8, 11, 17, 19, 21, 25, 32, 35, 36, 37, 38, 39, 41, 42, 43, 44, 45, 46, 51, 53, 57, 59, 60, 72, 73, 77, 80, 81, 83, 89, 91, 93, 95

prophets, 2, 3, 6, 8, 9, 13, 14, 16, 17, 18, 19, 20, 22, 23, 25, 27, 32, 33, 36, 39, 40, 41, 42, 43, 46, 47, 50, 53, 57, 58, 62, 65, 69, 72, 74, 75, 76, 82, 84, 85, 88, 89, 93, 94, 95

prosper, 5, 32, 42, 71, 76

prosperity, 46, 63, 64, 65, 66, 68, 69

protection, 25, 67

protector, 24

Psalmist, 76

publicly, 74

pure, 8, 24

pure vessel, 8

purpose, 3, 87

Q

question, 7, 17, 46, 47, 54, 58, 59, 76, 81, 85

R

races, 27

racism, 27

rallying, 45

rampant, 58

reactions, 88

reality, 1, 2, 9, 15, 16, 17, 20, 21, 23, 29, 33, 40, 43, 46, 47, 48, 49, 50, 52, 59, 65, 66, 71, 93

realm, 20, 36

reason, 2, 11, 46, 56, 69, 80, 85

reasoning, 56

rebellion, 22

reference, 80
reflection, 4, 17, 31, 32, 57, 64
refusal, 38
reject, 2
rejection, 2, 46
rejections, 2
rejects, 12
relationally, 16
relationships, 2, 17, 18, 31, 50
release, 67
relevant, 42, 69, 72
rendered, 16, 69
repent, 80, 81, 82, 84
repents, 61
repetition, 6
reproach, 92
reproduces, 73
rescue, 48
resilient, 3
respecter, 29
responsibility, 13, 31, 39, 49, 54, 57, 64
responsible, 20, 31
restless, 23
restored, 45, 54, 59
revelation, 5, 15, 20, 55, 60, 63, 72, 76
revelations, 3
Revivals, 95
rewards, 2
rich, 54, 55
ridicule, 92

righteous, 76, 83
righteousness, 45
road, 2, 81
role, 36, 44, 58

S

sabotage, 69
saints, 2
salvation, 77, 84
Samuel, 54, 80, 81, 82, 83, 84, 85, 89
satan, 10, 17
Satan, 16, 19, 20, 21, 23, 60, 63, 64, 67, 68, 88
Saul, 80, 81, 82, 83, 84, 85
schedule, 46, 81
schemes, 16, 20
search, 66
season, 32
see, 4, 5, 9, 10, 11, 13, 16, 17, 18, 19, 20, 21, 28, 29, 30, 38, 39, 40, 43, 45, 47, 48, 52, 53, 54, 55, 57, 60, 62, 65, 66, 68, 74, 76, 77, 80, 81, 84, 88, 89, 91, 92, 93
seed, 63, 64, 68
seeing, 11, 21, 53, 57, 78
seek, 7, 10, 13, 19, 49, 91, 94
self-acceptance, 38
self-awareness, 2, 36
selfish, 8
selfishness, 17, 55, 60
self-isolation, 37
senses, 11

sensitive, 73, 90
sensitivity, 25, 73, 78
serious issues, 8
servant, 19, 21, 43, 45, 59, 61
servants, 61, 66, 78, 81
serves, 77, 95
servitude, 45, 46, 56, 59, 75, 88, 89
shame, 67, 68
sharpen, 82
shortcomings, 18
shot, 45
showers, 46
sick, 23
sickness, 50
significant, 7, 15, 75, 88
sin, 17, 22, 23, 68, 84
singers, 72, 74
situation, 6, 25, 30, 42, 56, 80, 82, 91
skillful, 73
skin, 20
snare, 69
Social media, 2
social standards, 36
society, 37, 78, 95
sold, 73, 74, 75
Solomon, 75, 77
solution, 48
song, 73
soul, 1, 2, 3, 4, 5, 10, 11, 12, 13, 15, 17, 18, 20, 22, 24, 26, 28, 29, 30, 31, 32, 33, 35, 36, 37, 38, 39, 40, 41, 42, 43, 44, 45, 46,

47, 48, 50, 51, 52, 53, 54, 56, 57, 58, 60, 61, 62, 63, 64, 65, 66, 67, 68, 69, 70, 71, 72, 73, 74, 75, 76, 77, 78, 79, 80, 81, 82, 83, 84, 85, 86, 87, 89, 90, 92, 94

souls., 3, 56, 68, 85

south, 67

sowed, 63, 64

speak, 1, 7, 12, 29, 81, 83

spectrum, 88

spirit, 11, 12, 13, 20, 29, 30, 35, 48, 53, 62, 63, 64, 65, 68, 82, 84, 88

Spirit, 11, 12, 13, 22, 30, 66, 73, 78, 89

spiritists, 79

spiritual, 3, 19, 20, 31, 60

spiritually, 16, 88

spoiled, 58

stability, 32, 69, 92

stature, 55

status, 2, 37, 38, 53, 54, 55, 65, 70, 75, 84

steadfast, 7, 28

storms, 28, 46

strategy, 16

strength, 2, 3, 19, 20, 24, 41

stress, 28, 73

Stress, 28

strong, 19, 57, 81, 87

strongholds, 18, 19

struggle, 4, 6, 7, 15, 30, 46, 47, 48, 50, 73

struggling, 62, 65

study, 1, 10, 16, 72, 76

stumbling block, 88

subconscious, 6, 7, 23, 28, 50
subcultures, 34, 35, 39, 42, 43
submission, 6, 69, 78, 83
Submission, 67
submit, 1, 5, 9, 13, 41, 67, 69
submitted, 37, 40, 43, 60, 66, 68
succeed, 21
success, 2, 6
suffering, 29
suffocate, 18
suggestions, 23
sun, 85
supernatural, 24, 46
support, 74
surprises, 46
surrender, 6
synonym, 88

T

talk, 2, 11, 18, 43, 54, 82
tasting, 11
teach, 17, 22, 77, 95
temper, 8
temptation, 16, 24
terms, 9, 83
test, 74, 78, 80, 81
tests, 83, 86
thief, 69
thoughts, 7, 19, 22, 23, 33, 47, 48, 93

time, 1, 2, 3, 5, 8, 12, 16, 20, 23, 37, 38, 41, 46, 55, 61, 69, 71, 74, 76, 77, 84, 90
tools, 31
torment, 18, 19
train, 47
traitor, 90
translated, 12
transmits, 11, 12
trauma, 93
traveler, 54
trials, 81
Trinity, 62, 63, 64, 66, 67, 68, 69, 80, 83
trophies, 3
trouble, 26, 28, 81
troublesome, 15
trumpets, 74
trust, 2, 24, 40, 81, 93
truth, 9, 20, 23, 24, 29, 30, 42, 43, 77, 78, 82, 84

U

unbelief, 19, 67
undeniable, 34, 66
understanding, 5, 8, 10, 18, 19, 24, 37, 47, 48, 64, 67, 69, 95
unfair, 46, 49
unfaithful, 85
unfinished, 47, 57, 59
ungodly, 80
unique, 6, 42, 59
unison, 66

unknown, 70, 72, 73, 74, 77, 78
unrelenting, 17
unseen, 1, 2, 4, 5, 7, 9, 10, 11, 13, 20, 64, 68
Unseen, 1, 2, 3, 4
unstable, 32, 58, 59
untruths, 16
Uriah, 55, 61
USA, 95

V

validation, 12
veil, 28
vineyards, 70
virtually, 73
visible, 15, 22
visionary, 72
visions, 72
vocally, 73
voice, 22, 78

W

walked, 17, 43, 66
wander, 22
war, 1, 2, 4, 6, 8, 9, 10, 11, 12, 13, 14, 15, 16, 17, 18, 19, 21, 22, 31, 33, 52, 54, 56, 57, 64, 72, 84, 89
warfare, 22, 27, 31, 33, 53, 58, 68
watchman, 28, 52, 59, 77, 82
watchmen, 65

water, 32
weak, 1, 84
weakness, 41, 76
wealth, 50, 55, 65
weapons, 48
Where Eagles Fly Fellowship Inc, 95
wicked, 63, 71, 76
wife, 55, 61, 95
will,, 5, 6, 7, 10, 12, 18, 37, 87
wisdom, 6, 25, 41, 77, 90
witchcraft, 79
witches, 80
witness, 18, 69
wizards, 81
wonder, 8, 9, 12, 17, 27, 80, 84
wondered, 6, 71
Word of God, 6, 28, 40, 48
work, 1, 2, 6, 7, 9, 10, 14, 18, 23, 24, 35, 37, 40, 41, 42, 45, 48, 49, 50, 54, 59, 60, 61, 64, 66, 69, 71, 72, 73, 74, 76, 85, 90
world, 2, 5, 13, 14, 16, 20, 21, 22, 23, 24, 25, 27, 28, 30, 31, 33, 39, 40, 41, 47, 49, 53, 67, 74, 77, 78, 82
worry, 33, 67, 68, 74
worship, 24, 30, 73, 78
worth, 3
worthy, 24, 78
wounded, 26, 30, 32, 33
wreck, 81, 84
writing, 96

Z

Zachariah, 77

www.ingramcontent.com/pod-product-compliance
Lightning Source LLC
Chambersburg PA
CBHW072036110526
44592CB00012B/1448